Contact! Britain!

Contact! Britain!

A Memoir

Nancy Miller Livingston Stratford

California, USA, 2010

Edited by Margaret Miller

Cover and interior design by Marc C. Lee

Printed in the United States of America

To my dear father

Contents

Prologue

How did I get here?

It was a fleeting thought as I banked into the cloud layer, back to what I hoped would be clearer skies.

The English weather, as usual, was atrocious: low "scud," dirty gray clouds meandering along the hillsides. But here and there was a spot of daylight, encouraging me to go ahead and deliver the Spitfire to its destination, like the Devil waving his hand to come on through. I hesitated and thought about turning around. Since I had no radio or formal instrument training, it was imperative that I keep visual contact with the ground. I struggled to see it, some 500-600 feet beneath me, and also glanced up to see what visibility I had ahead.

I had already slowed the Spit up a bit, but even then things happened too quickly. All of a sudden the Devil's spot disappeared, and in a flash I realized that I couldn't see anything as the clouds enveloped me. It was like being in a bowl of milk; not knowing which way was up or down. I knew I had to look at my instruments, but I involuntarily started a turn to the left. A blink of my eyes to the turn-and-bank indicator, which registered on my brain as being too steep—the artificial horizon showed a 60-degree bank, and the aircraft was going down on the rate-of-climb indicator. All of this seemed to happen in an instant. But into my mind came this crazy thought:

How did I get here?

Acknowledgements

I would like to thank my friend Ann Wilde, without whose encouragement and support this memoir would not have seen the light of day; my niece Peggy Miller, whose editing help has been invaluable; and Marc Lee, for his good counsel and invaluable help with the pictures, graphics, and production.

Introduction

I didn't keep a diary of my time in the Air Transport Auxiliary, or ATA – I wish I had. But I figured I should write something about my past three years in Britain for one main reason. When I return home, I want to say, "Here ya are, Pop! Just you read this and it will tell you what I've been doing lately. Don't ask me any questions until you've read it." That way, I figure I can save myself a lot of breath and repetition.

But then I found myself waiting so long in London for a boat trip home that, for lack of anything better to do, I decided to correct some of the grammar and spelling, put the account into chapter form, and perhaps have it published as one more of the multitude of books about what the Americans (and British) did in World War II.

This account has no literary flourishes, no events of great importance. It was written for fun for my father, Ray O. Miller. It's a book about one individual, mostly about flying, as that was my job.

"Contact!" is an aviation term used prior to starting an engine. After calling out "Contact!" the pilot switches on the magnetos, and the engine starts as the propeller is pulled through. Used figuratively, as here, it means the start of an adventure.

London, England
1945

I.

ATA? NEVER HEARD OF IT

When I visited my friend Jay that eventful afternoon in January 1942, I did not foresee the future as I have experienced it. I was bored. I had just seen the Long Beach, California, air officials about using women in the ferry command, and they had said politely, "No soap," looking at me with that peculiar gleam which men get when they think women should stay at home. So off I drove to Jay's, a cooling trip to the beach. During the conversation, I mentioned my irritation at the superior male Army air officials. Jay mused a moment, then asked suddenly,

"How would you like to ferry planes in England?"

I laughed in amusement. "Quit kidding. Gals just don't do things like that."

"Well," she continued, shrugging her shoulders, "I know English girls do it, and I know that there are some American women going over. I thought you might like it. It's all rather hush-hush now, but - well, really, would you like to do it?"

"Jay", I sputtered, still disbelieving, "if there's such a service, I'd like to know something about it - but I still think you're kidding."

"OK, I'll call up Polly and ask her about it. She's going in the first group, and maybe I can get some more information from her."

Polly was out, and Jay didn't know much about it except that men and women flew all sorts of trainers, pursuits (fighters), and bombers (I had to laugh again in disbelief) from factories to squadrons as a part of the Air Transport Auxiliary. About twenty-five women pilots were being recruited by Jacqueline Cochran. Pay – maybe $300 per month. Experience needed – at least 300 hours and a flight check in an AT-6 in Montreal. Age – 21-35. Education – at least a high-school graduate. So far, so good. Jay said to write to Miss Cochran, which I did. I received a telegram from her secretary, Mary Nicholson, to call Miss Cochran at such and such a hotel in Los Angeles on such and such a day, which I did. Appointment for interview. Interview. Miss Cochran was in bed as a result of typhoid injections, which didn't agree with her.

"Did you get a telegram from me last July?" she asked.

"No." I had heard about that from Jay. Miss Cochran had sent "feelers" in July 1941 to all women pilots having at least 200 hours. "Perhaps that's because I didn't have 200 hours at that time," I explained.

"How many do you have now?"

"About 450, mostly from piling up hours for my commercial and instructor's licensing and instructing."

"Well, that's good. I want my pilots to have recent experience, if possible."

After asking only a few more questions, she gave me an application blank and telephone number. I called that number several days later and was placed on the list in the fifth, or next-to-last, group to go to Montreal. It was impossible to believe that women flew Spitfires and – what was that other pursuit? oh yes, the

Hurricane – and two-engine bombers. And I couldn't help but laugh when Miss Cochran said that the English called the practice of takeoffs and landings "circuits and bumps"! "Bumps" indeed! But that was an accurate description, I must say.

I didn't go to Montreal until the middle of July 1942.

When I saw Miss Cochran in February, I had just finished instructing one Civilian Pilot Training program and was on a couple of weeks' vacation. While waiting, I had put in five hours in the Link Trainer (simulator), that tricky little "blackout box" which at first is so confusing. I stepped into the contraption, set about two feet above ground level, started the motor, and then the fun began.

"Steady, you're diving. Not too much stick, watch your airspeed. You're slipping. Watch those instruments."

I **was** watching those instruments – they were blurring before my eyes. This Link only had the elementary instruments: turn-and-bank, climb-and-descent, airspeed indicator (ASI), altimeter, clock. No artificial horizon, no directional gyro, as with later models. But it seemed as if I were looking at 10,000 things. Nothing remained constant. Airspeed 160 miles an hour – normal. I didn't do a thing, I thought, but suddenly the ASI was down to 110. I shoved forward, waited a second, pulled back. ASI 130, 140, 150, 160, 170, 180 – golly, would it never stop? Back on the stick more – ah! 180, 170, 160 – I began to relax.

"Watch the ball. Keep it in the center," came the words through the phones. I switched my popping eyes to the turn-and-bank. Whew, quite a slip! Straighten up – atta gal. ASI – 120. My gosh, how the devil did that get there? Stick forward – 130, 140. Good night, now I'm turning! Would I ever get this darn plane steady?

So it went. I was a wreck at the end of that first half hour but had not let the ASI drop to the fatal 80-mph mark where the machine simulates a spin. Several days later, though, I saw to my horror the ASI going down rapidly – 110, 100, 90. I shoved forward hard, but it was too late. The turn-and-bank went screwball, and the vertical descent dropped quickly to 1,000 feet per minute or so. I was in a spin. I could feel only a slight pressure to one side of the cockpit, and my head felt a bit light. Concentrating hard, I finally brought it out. Of course, the instructor gave me no help at all when needed and just grinned when I sheepishly stepped out. Drat some instructors!

I went back to Bishop, where I had five boys in the primary CPT course. One had had previous experience, but I didn't know it at the time. I wondered why he was doing so well on landings. With 17 hours behind him, about 10 solo, naturally he progressed quickly. I thought I had a bright student, which I did, but I felt my ego deflate when I finally looked at his previous record. I had secret hopes that my teaching was inspirational or something, but no, he just had 17 hours to help him out!

I found out why when I first soloed, my instructor looked so relieved afterwards. Heavens, I was doing the solo, not he. But this time, I was on the ground watching my fledglings. Four of them soloed in one afternoon, one after the other. All of them did a dandy job, but I was pretty jittery that evening. I wonder what it is that makes an instructor so keen and yet so fearful of his student's solo? There is nothing more satisfying (aside from one's own super-duper 3-point landing) than seeing a first solo by someone you have instructed.

You sit or stand by the landing area and hope that big mutt in the 765 does not cut in on your boy. After all, you're pretty proud of Bob and want him to have a little elbow room for a nice approach and landing. Golly, wouldn't it be awful if they collided? Quit thinking things like that! OK, but if anything happens. . . . You shift your weight nervously and practically talk him through every move.

"Don't skid in that turn. Keep 'er coming in easily. You're high, bring back that throttle. Come on, get 'er down. My golly, you'll overshoot. Ah, that's better. Down, down, but not too fast, and for heaven's sake, don't dive it into the ground! Now level off. Oops, too much speed. Hold 'er off. Easy does it. Get that stick back, keep that plane off the ground. Come on, get that darn stick back! Ah, that's it. A beauty!"

A heavy sigh of relief as Bob stops after landing. "Not bad, not bad," you mutter. Loosening your hands from your jacket, you find they're wet with perspiration. Funny, Bob was making the solo, not you.

"Nice job he did," says a fellow instructor nearby, and inside you feel warm and proud.

It's a sort of tradition for solo students to treat their instructors to something "stronger than ginger-ale." Not being a drinker or a smoker, I presented the boys with a quandary. Finally three of them treated me at my favorite hangout, the soda fountain. The other two bought a lovely identification bracelet with wings on one side, my initials and commercial license number on the other. I prized that greatly. I used to fiddle with it and remember the grand time I had with that group. I must have fiddled too much, for one day in England, a year later, one of the links broke and the bracelet was lost.

But I haven't forgotten the memories: the one-main-street country town Bishop, the one cinema, the soda fountain, the night club with its amusing three-piece orchestra and various floorshows. The roller-skating couple – there for a week's engagement – were marvelous, and at the completion of their routine, the man would whirl one member of the audience around. I did it once and wobbled unsteadily back to the table amidst very rude laughter, I thought. How do those skaters ever keep their balance? There were juke boxes too, and "Deep in the Heart of Texas" always reminds me of Bishop, not Texas. When I left for Montreal, the boys chipped in and gave me a lovely sweater. Instructing does have its rewards sometimes.

Before reporting to Montreal, I took a trip to New York, visiting relatives along the way. In New York, I met Mary Nicholson, secretary to Miss Cochran, who gave me more details of my future trip. I recognized a name on the list of women to report in June. I asked Mary to show me her application picture. Yes, it was she. After all these years! Kay Van Doozer had taught me some history and English back in 1929 or 1930. What a small world!

Mary Nicolson herself qualified in the last group, resigned her position, and went to England. She made many friends and enjoyed the work and England greatly. Miss Pauline Gower, commandant of women, even sent a little personal note to her family, and Mary was thrilled that they would receive a letter from her chief. Several days later, she was ferrying her first job after finishing training. The propeller flew off, and Mary crashed. I thought of that kind note which would arrive many days after a sudden heart-breaking cable.

When I flew back commercially from New York to Oakland, I had to laugh. The blinds were drawn according to orders, and it made me a little peeved, as I had learned to fly out of this same airport which now I wasn't permitted to see.

During the remaining three weeks of freedom, I shopped, packed, and loafed. I bought an amazing array of canned goods (we all thought England was starving), underclothes (including heavy winter woolies), shoes, and other necessities. Unwisely, I didn't buy many brown silk or rayon stockings, which were as good as gold, but I did take many black ones for my uniform. I only used a few pairs and sold the rest.

My canned goods stood up well and increased in value as time passed. Most of the items were not available in England or had very high point values. Peaches, apricots, and pears ranked high; baked beans, spaghetti, lima beans, and peas were all much appreciated. The one important item to me was a little bottle of real French dressing, which I used sparingly for seven months until I could squeeze nothing more from it. I filled up a large old-fashioned trunk plus three suitcases with clothes, canned goods, and so forth. But I learned fast, once in England. Traveling light is a blessing and an art; once accomplished, it saves a good many headaches. I was slow, but finally I sent my trunk home after my second year and lived happily from the three suitcases.

After packing, I took in the beach, getting a last glimpse of the good ol' California sun, and guzzled real ice cream milkshakes; then on to Montreal. Until the telegram came, I never believed that I would actually get to go. It just didn't seem real. I had that same feeling three years later when I left England. Because each phase of my life seemed complete and the future was unknown, the feeling of reality was nil. You want to go and yet you don't, and the uncertainty of waiting almost seems to blot out the future. But here it was. I said goodbye to Dad on June 11th, the day before my 23rd birthday. The train rumbled off, and I began to imagine what the next few years would bring. As if I were in an airplane ready to go, I silently said to myself, "Contact! Britain!" and the adventure began.

Air Transport Auxiliary (ATA)

The ATA was a British civilian outfit whose primary job, before being demobilized in November 1945, was to ferry all sorts of aircraft for the Royal Air Force, Fleet Air Arm (Navy), and Coastal Command, mainly within the limits of the United Kingdom. It was responsible to the Air Ministry through its parent organization, the British Overseas Airways Corporation (BOAC).

The ATA was formed in September 1939; it was made up of a handful of male pilots who were too old or medically unit for combat flying. In January 1940, the first eight British women were admitted but were restricted to small, light trainers for a year before being allowed to fly fighters and bombers. Overall, between 1939 and 1945 there were about 1300 pilots in the ATA, of whom about 150 to 160 were women.

Each pilot was assigned to a station or "pool." He or she was a first pilot, captain of the ship; there were no co-pilots, although trained ATA flight engineers (non-pilots) flew in the four-engine bombers, the C-47s, and the B-25s. Pilots never knew what kind of plane they would have next.

Britain is a small territory, so you can't fly long without running out of land. That means many trips were very short, sometimes ten to fifteen minutes, often between twenty-five to forty-five minutes and seldom more than an hour. Pilots could fly five different types of aircraft within one day, from light trainers to B-24s, and only log about two or three hours. Yet the experience gained was much more valuable than the actual time or than a single three-hour hop in one plane.

There were no radios in the aircraft and therefore no instrument flying, although it was impossible to fly in Britain without running inadvertently into instrument conditions. The British weather, so unpredictable, caused a good many precautionary landings, and it could take four or five days to complete an ordinary one-hour delivery flight.

Training, except for a few people, was more "conversion" or "transition" than actual instruction. Before entering the ATA, most pilots had had at least 50 hours of flight time, some up to 1,000. Training consisted of dual checkouts on perhaps four or five single-engine planes, ranging from a low-wing tandem trainer through a bi-plane, a high-wing cabin plane, a high-powered trainer, and a fighter. The twin-engine checkouts would be in three or four types: a trainer, a heavier transport, and a tricycle-gear plane. Outside of these, new types were flown solo the first time up with only the help of specially issued ATA handling notes, as forty-one of my fifty ATA types were.

There are very few organizations in the world that have given the individual pilot so much leeway as the ATA, not only as to flying but also in choosing his or her own time during doubtful weather. The accumulation of training and experience soon gave the pilot the confidence and ability to fly all types of aircraft. The handling notes were so well prepared that the pilot could absorb every detail concerning ferrying and emergencies from them.

In 1942, Miss Jacqueline Cochran—who followed Amelia Earhart as the foremost woman aviatrix of the time, establishing a number of speed records and winning races—asked for some American women volunteers to join the ATA pilots, at the request and permission of the British government. Twenty-four women went to Britain that year, with three coming over later on their own initiative. That was several months before Mrs. Nancy Love began the Women's Auxiliary Flying Service (WAFS), which was later, under Miss Cochran, to become the Women's Airforce Service Pilots (WASP). We had the British women who preceded us in the ATA to thank for proving that women could fly all types of aircraft, which eventually included the four-engine bombers. The success of the British and then the American and other women in the ATA was the forerunner of and blueprint for the women's organizations, the WAFS and the WASP, in the US.

If you forget what the ATA stands for, remember that some say it stands for "Anything to Anywhere," and some called us the "ATTA Girls." But most remember us all, regardless of gender, as the "Ancient and Tattered Airmen."

```
CLASS OF SERVICE                                    1200    SYMBOLS
This is a full-rate     WESTERN                             DL=Day Letter
Telegram or Cable-                                          NT=Overnight Telegram
gram unless its de-                                         LC=Deferred Cable
ferred character is in-  UNION                              NLT=Cable Night Letter
dicated by a suitable
symbol above or pre-    R. B. WHITE    NEWCOMB CARLTON   J. C. WILLEVER    Ship Radiogram
ceding the address.     PRESIDENT      CHAIRMAN OF THE BOARD  FIRST VICE-PRESIDENT
```

The filing time shown in the date line on telegrams and day letters is STANDARD TIME at point of origin.   Time of receipt is STANDARD TIME at point of destination

BAS12 282/281 NT 1/165/164=NEWYORK NY JAN 23

ANN WATSON WOOD =   1942 JAN 24 AM 8 14

    WALDOBORO ME=

CONFIDENTIAL= ON BEHALF BRITISH AIR TRANSPORT AUXILIARY I
AM WIRING ALL THE WOMEN PILOTS WHOSE ADDRESSES AVAILABLE
TO ASK IF YOU WOULD BE WILLING TO VOLUNTEER FOR SERVICE WITH
A NUCLEUS TO CONSTITUTE INITIAL CONTINGENT OF NEWLY=FORMED
AMERICAN WOMEN'S SECTION OF ATA FOR SERVICE IN BRITISH
ISLES= REQUIREMENTS COMPRISE REGULAR ATA EXAMINATION
INCLUDING FLIGHT TEST AND PHYSICAL EXAMINATION IN MONTREAL=
IF AFTER I HAVE INTERVIEWED YOU YOU ARE ACCEPTABLE YOU
WILL RECEIVE YOUR TRANSPORTATION TO MONTREAL AND MAINTENANCE
WHILE THERE= IF IN MONTREAL YOU PASS YOUR FLIGHT TEST AND
ALL OTHER REQUIREMENTS YOU WILL BE SENT TO ENGLAND=
REMUNERATION SAME AS PAID ENGLISH WOMEN ATA PILOTS ABROAD
AS WELL AS ADDITIONAL ACCUMULATION IN DOLLARS AT HOME=
SUBSTANTIAL INSURANCE AND TWO WAY TRANSPORTATION FROM YOUR
HOME TO ENGLAND= RANKS WOULD BE SAME GENERALLY AS ENGLISH
ATA WOMEN PILOTS= UNIFORMS FURNISHED BY ATA= BELIEVE WE WILL
GET ORGANIZED TO LEAVE ABOUT MARCH FIRST= EVERY FRONT NOW
OUR FRONT AND FOR THOSE DESIRING QUICK ACTIVE SERVICE SHORT=

THE COMPANY WILL APPRECIATE SUGGESTIONS FROM ITS PATRONS CONCERNING ITS SERVICE

The telegram that started it all

1942 JAN 24 AM 8 13

:OF ACTUAL COMBAT BUT INCLUDING FLIGHT EXPERIENCE WITH COMBAT
PLANES THIS SERVICE ABROAD SEEMS IDEAL CHANCE. I HAVE BEEN
ASSURED BY THOSE IN AUTHORITY THAT WOMEN WILL NOT BE USED
FOR FERRYING OR ANY ORGANIZED FLYING DUTIES IN AMERICA FOR
MANY MONTHS. IF INTERESTED AND SO I WILL KNOW THE NUMBER
AVAILABLE AND THEIR LOCATION FOR MY ITINERARY OF INTERVIEWS
PLEASE WIRE ME 630 FIFTH AVENUE NEWYORKCITY AND YOU WILL
RECEIVE LETTER WITH MORE DETAILS. OFFICIAL PRESS RELEASES
HAVE BEEN MADE BY THE BRITISH AIR COMMISSION AND YOU ARE
REQUESTED TO RELEASE NO PUBLICITY AS A RESULT OF THIS
TELEGRAM. IF YOU HAVE NAMES OF ANY WOMEN PILOTS I HAVE
MISSED PASS ALONG YOUR TELEGF'M. CORDIAL REGARDS=
    JACQUELINE COCHRAN.

36

Contact! Britain!

II.

THE BIG JUMP

<u>Montreal</u>. It didn't seem different from the States, except for French being spoken by many inhabitants. When the aircraft was serviceable and the weather passable, the five of us flew; otherwise we just sat or shopped. On June 19th, I had my first taste of the AT-6 Harvard, an advanced single-engine trainer. It was a big jump to this 600-horsepower noisy beauty, especially after 65-horsepower trainers. My goodness, the gadgets! Landing gear, power knob, flaps, pitch lever, throttle, carburetor heat control, inertia starter, wobble pump and so forth; very confusing. Give me back my Luscombe!

Captain Harry Smith of the ATA and I battled our way around. It was rather amusing to see the little Harvard amongst all the twin and four-engine planes, and we had to follow their large circuit patterns. Our check consisted entirely of "circuits and bumps," and these were always crosswind for some reason. The wind was never right. I recall that the plane appeared to be a mass of gadgets, and the tricky crosswind kept my confidence at lowest ebb.

But I haven't forgotten the thrill of that first solo and using radio for the first time. My stage fright was tremendous, but the control tower operator put me at ease with his soothing patter and the plane, fortunately, behaved itself. I still wonder how I ever passed that stage, but I did.

On July 9th, Opal Anderson of Chicago and I set sail for England. She had passed in the fourth group but returned to the States for a month. Why we boarded the freighter Winnipeg II at Montreal, I don't know. It took us nine days to reach Halifax, loading up with various war commodities along the way. On a train, it's a boring, rough trip of 24 hours or so. Still, 24 hours is better than nine days.

There is an endless stretch of water between Halifax and Liverpool. There were several alarms that German submarines were near, which increased everyone's heart rate - but there were no attacks. Then suddenly a coast line appeared - Ireland. The RAF boys aboard- having completed their training in Canada- thought only of coming home, Opal and I of a strange land. One consolation: our languages were the same – almost.

Soon our "Mae Wests" (life vests) were left on the bunks, and we chugged into the harbor. The small freighter tied up and, from the top deck, I saw Miss Cochran far below waiting for us. I said goodbye to the captain who, with the chief engineer, had given Opal and me some hot battles in rummy. We were all relieved that the slow, uneventful but uncertain convoy trip was over.

A few months later I shuddered when I heard that our good ol' Winnipeg II had been torpedoed and sunk on its return trip to the States.

III.

SO THIS IS ENGLAND

Liverpool. I had heard of it, vaguely. The first thing I saw reminded me that I was in war-torn England: Barrage balloons-many, many of them- floating lazily in the skies at about 500 to 1,500 feet to fend off low-level airplane attacks. I originally had thought they were to tangle up high-flying bombers and that they were raised to 10,000 feet or so. On the taxi ride into the city, we saw bombed-out areas, whole blocks gone, the debris cleared away but the foundations jutting grotesquely out into space, buildings gutted and now only skeletons.

We stayed at the Adelphi Hotel that night, where I learned that orange squash was not a vegetable but an orangeade. When the waitress asked me if I wanted squash, I said "Yes," thinking of the yellow vegetable. When I inquired about its not coming, she pointed to the orangeade she had brought and remarked, "There is your orange squash." Naturally, I was somewhat confused until Miss Cochran laughingly explained. That wasn't the only time I ever blushed about language differences!

Learning British English

As I learned later, if you want suspenders, be sure to ask for "braces" or else you'll get garters! A nice open toasted-cheese sandwich is lovely, but you won't get one unless you ask for "Welsh rarebit." "Cookies" are small cakes, "biscuits" are our cookies, and a "scone" is a flat pastry. A "tube" may be a subway or a radio valve. "Walking sticks" are our canes, and the British use them a great deal. Somebody was insulted when an English lass told her she was so "homely." In Britain, that's a compliment and is not meant in the ruder descriptive sense, as Americans use it. If you ask for a rest room, as I did once, you're ushered into a huge lounge. To go to the john, you should say you need to "spend a penny." Somehow, when I try politely to get to the john, I often ask if there's any place to wash my hands. "Certainly, madam," I'm told, and then I'm taken to a place where I **can** wash my hands but where there's no toilet around. They separate these two things so much that you must be quite unabashed and ask for exactly what you want!

However, they can throw you off completely with the ever-present "You caaan't miss it," which always ends any directions you're given. They say, "Turn right, turn left, past the White Horse (a pub), you caaan't miss it." Invariably, you miss it.

There is one British expression I've learned that nearly everyone agrees is excellent. I know I shall continue to use it back in the States, as it fits so many occasions. It is "You've had it." "What have I had?" you ask perplexed. Well, if you miss the streetcar or train, "You've had it!" If you don't have enough points for a steak, "You've had it!" If there's no steak anyhow, "You've had it!" If your horse finishes fourth on a show ticket, "You've had it!" If you spill the gravy, "You've had it!" If Poppa says no more allowance, "You've had it!" And if I don't get off the subject, "I'll have had it!"

"Good show" is another British expression which has amused me. I resisted it for a couple of years, saying the American "good" or "good thing." However, one is bound to acquire some expressions after living with them so long. "Good show" or "wizard show" is applied to anything that is done well. The latter expression is used mainly by the RAF in reference to successful air-raid missions. It took me a long while to use "good show" easily, but it took even longer to overcome it, much to the amusement and kidding of my American friends.

We also had our first air raid alert in Liverpool, and I could swear the siren was right underneath my bed! Never have I heard such a wailing, and the fact that it was associated not with fire trucks at home but with possible bombers made my heart pound furiously as I ducked under the covers and then under the bed. "Wailing Willie" or "Moaning Minnie," as the British called the sirens, were very apt names. About ten minutes later, I sheepishly arose, put on my bathrobe, and went down to the basement. There were the other residents, in bathrobes too—and the bar was open!

London. Things happened quickly from Liverpool. A trip by train to London. Photographs for identification purposes. National identity cards, aliens' registration cards. Out to Maidenhead, the headquarters of the ATA for a medical check. To Luton, north of London, for training. Getting billets (housing). Attending ground school. Yes, it was all confusing. Out of it though, there were a few noticeable impressions.

First, the taxis. My first thought was of vintage 1930 and no hope of improvement. I had heard Britain was behind the times in many things, and here was one. The drivers were just as I had pictured. Old-timers, with large moustaches and broad accents that I could hardly understand. But I soon learned that the taxis slipped through traffic quickly and my, how those horseless buggies turned on a dime! Or should I say a six-pence?

That was another matter. Money. Why did the English waste so much copper in their pennies? That wasn't as much a concern to me, though, as making twelve pennies equal one shilling and twenty shillings equal a pound and distinguishing between two shillings (two-bob) and half-a-crown. Complications. Finally, I worked out the values fairly well, but it didn't prevent me from spending a pound (four dollars) just about the same as I would a dollar bill.

My third impression was the way cars sailed down the wrong side of the roads. That's another special English custom. I invariably leaned to the right as we swung the opposite way to go around a "round-about" or circle. We passed cars on the wrong side - everything was wrong, except that somehow the cars seldom collided.

Railroads were soon an old story, but the first time I saw Paddington station, I was downright disappointed. I was spoiled by our beautiful ones at home. This one had no signs for where to buy tickets, no directions for anything; the trains were surrounded by the platforms themselves, the station was dark and dirty, the roof had holes in it (bomb damage), and the few stores were cheerless, the people glum. Opal and I stood in line, which we learned was called a "queue," and bought tickets. There was no one to help with the baggage except a few women, fewer men, and seemingly no organization. The train compartments held eight each, each person quiet and unsmiling- a dismal atmosphere. The train started on time but arrived late. This, as I learned by experience, was the usual procedure.

Another thing I noticed was the lack of corner drug stores with soda fountains. There seemed to be few places to get a good snack; few clean, efficient cafes; no soda fountains as we know them. Their chemist (drug) stores were in the middle of the block, hard to find, selling little besides actual medical supplies, and there was no real ice cream anywhere. I had a taste of their "ices," which reminded me of dirty dishwater, and then these were banned altogether. It wasn't until 1945 that the ban was lifted, but they still did not have the variety or quality of the familiar American ice creams.

Opal and I had our medical checks and went to Luton for elementary training. It took a week to settle into billets, and three weeks of ground school nearly ruined our patience. Our billets were with private families, not in barracks.

As time went on, I got used to the food. I knew exactly what we would have each day. It wasn't bad, although cabbage and brussel sprouts became monotonous. Of course before I came over, I had expected to starve, so I had brought along quite a few cans. These I did not need but used only as luxuries. There was plenty of food but no variety.

Seasons became important. When cabbage and sprouts were in, that was that. When apples were ripe, we had baked apples, apple pies, apple tarts, applesauce, and raw apples. When beans and peas were in season, we had those exclusively. Strawberries, giant red juicy ones from southern England, ripened for about three weeks; by the end of that time, one would be pretty tired of them. Potatoes we never worried about, nor bread, as they were the filling-up commodities - especially boiled potatoes. However, most people had a decent diet, even if too starchy, and were far from starving.

Ground school consisted mainly of adjusting to British instruments, especially the big flat master compass, learning a bit of Morse code (I got up to all of three words per minute!), and reading RAF maps. We did a bit of navigational theory and plotted numerous courses on the maps for use later in our cross-country flights. These maps (with a scale of 4 miles to the inch) were full of detail, including all sorts of roads with each and every bend (an accomplishment in itself, for the British roads are anything but straight), woods and forests in exact outline, churches, lakes, streams, pubs, golf courses, race courses, mansions, castles – all in addition to the usual towns and railroads.

Handling Notes

"Handling notes" were comprehensive booklets on all of the 100+ types of aircraft that the ATA flew, which we read anytime we flew a new type. There was also the *Blue Bible*, a set of about 4" by 6" stiff paper pages fitted into two big rings so that the notes could be turned over easily. The *Bible* was about 1 ½ inches thick, with a sturdy blue protective cover, and would fit into the knee pocket of our flight overalls. All of the information one needed was printed on these cards, with general and emergency information and all the speeds and settings neatly and concisely available at a glance.

Flying Terminology

In flying, a number of terms are different in British English. "Petrol" is used instead of gasoline. "Coarse" and "fine" pitch are used instead of – well, I never can get high and low pitch straightened out myself. "Boost gauges" are used because the British don't use inches of manifold pressure. Takeoffs and landings, as I've said, are "circuits and bumps." Something written up as "U/S" is unserviceable. The "U/C" was the undercarriage or undercart—as we think of it, the landing gear or wheels. A "ropey" old aircraft was one that didn't fly very well. If you had an accident, you "pranged it."

Some of the ATA pilots put appropriate words to various tunes. One consisted of one verse of "Popeye, the Sailor Man"; the second verse was "My Bonnie Lies Over the Ocean"; and the third was "Bless Them All."

I am in the ATA
I break up whatever I may
I am what I am
And I prang what I can
Whatever they give me each day, Poop-Poop!

My Spitfire lies spread on the runway
My Walrus collapsed in the sea
I know there was never a pilot
Who broke up more aircraft than me.

Prang them all – prang them all
The large and the fast and the small
Prang all those Mossies and
Prang all those Spits
Prang all those Wimpies and bust them to bits.
Cause I'm tired and fed up with this war
And flying's becoming a bore.
I have notion I'll get my promotion.
Just because I prang them all.

Finally, the glorious day came: flying. The hardest part came in trying to make the map and what we saw 1,000 feet below agree. Somehow all the fields, woods, railroads looked the same. It was a great day when one could fly fifty miles without a map, for England is a very difficult place for navigation. We had no radio and therefore when really lost, we had to sit down at an airport to ask where we were – an embarrassing experience, to say the least!

(A sample from the A.T.A. "Bluebook" ferry handling notes, printed in small type on a 3 x 5 stiff card, and used for reference on every flight . Brief, important cards were written on every type of plane used by the A.T.A.)

MOSQUITO

Marks: I,II,III, IV,VI,VIII,IX,XII,XIII,XVI,XVII,XVIII,
 XIX,XX,XXV,XXVI,XXX, XXXIV,XXXV,XXXVI
Engines: Two Merlins. 2-speed or 2-speed 2-stage blowers.
 Some have injection carburettors.
                                      Fuel: 100 octane.
Propellers: Hydromatic,fully feathering. 4-bladed
 props will not feather.
U/C operation:
 Normal: Hydraulic. Pump on each engine. 3-position
  lever should return to neutral. Always move
  smartly to DOWN. Check green lights again
  after lowering flaps.
 Reserve: Hand pump with detachable handle. Instal on
  pump with jaw to starboard before starting.
  Select DOWN. Pump approximately 20 minutes to
  lower all wheels.
 Emergency: Lowers only through separate lines. First
  try to pump 25° flap, then push down valve
  (under rubber or screwed dural cap on some) at
  right of pilot's seat and operate hand pump.
  It does not lower tail wheel.
 Indicators: Two green lights, locked DOWN. Two red,
  in transit(or if throttle closedwith U/C
  not locked down). No lights, locked up.
  Warning horn. Mark XX has pictorial indicators.
 Safety locks: Locking caps with red flags must be re-
  placed by dustcaps before takeoff.

Flaps: Normal:
 Reserve: Same general idea as above.
 Emerg.:
Gills: Manual or pneumatic controlled by electric switches.
  Minimum air pressure:160 lbs/sq.in. Filter
  switch(if fitted) usually normal(out) for
  ferrying.
Tanks: (Number of tanks,where placed andcock controls,
  plus quantities.)
Starting: 24-volt direct. Dopers in nacelles. Etc.
Pressure cabin: (Special instructions.)

                    Flying Particulars
Takeoff:
 Booster pumps: Blowers: Boost: RPM: Mixture: Gills:
 "On",if fitted   M   +12 3000   Rich,
                                    if fitted Open

"Handling notes" for the DeHavilland Mosquito bomber

(page 1)

Takeoff:(con't)
Trim:
  Elevators: Rudder:and
  Neutral(or 1   aileron:
  division nose-   Neutral
  down:with flap)

Climb:(A.T.A.)
Boost:	RPM:	Gills:	Flaps:	Booster pumps:	ASI:
+6	2600	Open	UP	OFF(if fitted)	180 mph

A.T.A Cruise:
Boost:	RPM:	Mixture:	Gills:	ASI:	Consumption:
0	2300	Weak	Closed	190-230	45 gals/eng.hr.

Slow flying:
Boost:	RPM:	Mixture:	Gills:	Flaps:	ASI:
As re-quired.	2600	Rich	Watch temps.	30°	140 mph

Single-engine:
Boost:	RPM:	Mixture:	Gills:	Dead Prop:	ASI:
Level:+6	2600	Rich	Watch temps.	Feathered	180 mph
Climb: +9	2850	Rich	"	"	180 mph

Stall: Flaps and U/C UP: 122 mph. Flaps and U/C Down: 112 mph.
Glide: " : 150 mph.   " : 140 "

Approach and Land:
Flaps:	Effect:	Max.speed for flaps:	Final approach:	ASI:
DOWN	Powerful nose-up	Max.speed for U/C:	125 mph (with or	180 mph
		150 mph 180 mph	without static vent)	140

Warning: ASI in knots, 2) takeoff to avoid swing, open slowly,fol-
  of run, 3) drop tank fitted, max. speed 250. ETC.

################

Frequently, this is all the information we had about an airplane

(Page 2)

Well do I remember the Miles Magister, fondly called the "Maggie," a 125-horsepower low-wing trainer. I had an American instructor, a dandy fellow, and at least I could understand him through the intercom system. That is, I heard parts of his speeches, for somehow I could never hear through those earphones well. Captain Ben Warne would ask; "What is the name of this place?" to check up on my navigation. I'd yell back;

"What did you say?" He'd repeat.

I'd yell back again, "What did you say? I can't hear you." He'd maneuver around in the front cockpit to eye me, press the mouthpiece closer and yell once more.

"Oh," I'd sigh feebly, looking down to see nothing but odd-shaped fields.

"What place?" I'd inquire. He would look down, open his mouth, think better about it, and shrug his shoulders while I fervently hoped my next checkpoint would turn up soon. I had no idea which town we had just passed.

Ben Warne

Captain Ben Warne, my first instructor in Maggies, was presented with a medal – the MBE (Member of the British Empire). It was well earned, too. It seems that he was instructor in a Hudson with Jane Plant of Maryland when one of the engines caught fire in the air. What with the fire and smoke, it was necessary to get down immediately if not quicker. Ben landed and jumped out to safety. Then he realized that Jane wasn't there, so he went back into the smoke and burning wreckage and pulled her out. There was some rumor that he was going to measure his lady students' hips after that, for it was a tight squeeze through the side window, although Jane is not large. Anyhow, although a bit burned, they both returned after a couple of months' rest in the States and continued their duties.

Earlier, Ben had had a trip home scheduled in 1943 for leave. A week later we heard that his boat had been torpedoed. For days we waited for word, but none came. Finally when all hope had been given up, we heard that he and some others had been taken from an island to Portugal by a small ship after spending eleven days on a raft. The raft navigator did some dead-reckoning, guessing that was so close they hit the small island within an hour of his estimated time. That was real navigation, especially without all the new-fangled aids. Ben vowed that he wouldn't go home again until the war was over – too much danger! So he kept flying until the Hudson accident sent him home for a rest (safely, this time!)

It was good flying weather that month between August 28th and September 28th– that is, as English weather goes– and we were kept busy flying about the country for practice. Shifting to the Hart, an old biplane with a very narrow undercarriage (landing gear), the old fighter (pursuit) made us tremble in our boots. Every landing was made with a prayer that the wheels wouldn't buckle or that she wouldn't ground loop (a circular swerve off the runway). The Hart was a first-line fighter plane back around 1930, but now the de-rated 450-hp machine introduced new pilots to a little more horsepower and how to land when you were sitting three stories up. Also, instructors liked to play, so aerobatics were included unofficially.

My session of aerobatics was a bit expensive. Knowing the reputation of my instructor, an Englishman, I left everything except my locker key in my locker. After the first few slow rolls, I didn't care much for the scenery. I was not sick, but I simply couldn't get my straps tight, and the sensation of hanging half in and half out didn't appeal to me. Then "deah ol' chappie" Pennington-Leigh started a tremendous dive onto the airfield. I saw the ASI pass 250 mph, then off the clock at 275, which was far too fast for this old battlewagon. We must have hit 300 mph as we began to pull out. Up we went, then over slowly, returning right side up but heading practically straight up. Then he "cut the gun" (closed the throttle) and said,

"All yours. Force land onto the field."

After recuperating on land for a bit, I found that my locker key had made its exit from my pocket. Seeing P.-Leigh a few minutes later, I found him very dejected.

"Why so blue?" I asked.

"Well, I lost 30-bob ($6.00) in change out of my pocket, and I've only found one penny on top of the hangar," he answered sadly. Ah yes, quite an expensive trip!

Mr. Pennington-Leigh

Mr. Pennington-Leigh was British, as you may guess from the double-barreled name. He was very tall and straight. In fact, his back ran straight up without a curve from his shoulder to his cranium. And to make things complete, he had a real British moustache – sweeping far out into sharp points beyond each cheek. The students in the Maggies used to tell me that they, sitting in the rear seat, could use Mr. P-Leigh's moustache as an artificial horizon. No fooling!

Captain Fairweather

Another character I heard a lot about was Captain Fairweather. He once delivered two pilots to their destinations whose last names were Raines and Shine. Pilots Black, White, and Brown were also on that flight.

An old-time British pilot with umpteen hundreds of hours, he once had to collect a group of very senior BOAC (British Overseas Airways Corporation) pilots. Now, it's the custom that the senior pilot always takes over the plane. Captain Fairweather, at that time only a second officer, picked up these individuals in a twin-engine Anson. As they got in, they began comparing hours to find out who was the most senior. In the meantime, Fairweather taxied quietly down to the takeoff point. Finally, he turned around and asked who the senior pilot was. One pilot jumped up anxiously and said he was, walking forward. Captain Fairweather asked:

"I was wondering if you could answer me a troublesome question. Could you tell me on which engine I should take off?" With that, he flew the plane home.

Captain Fairweather was noted for his smoking. Very sloppy, he was, with ashes always down his protruding front. Finally the CO issued an order that nobody was to smoke in aircraft (a British rule generally), upon penalty of instant dismissal. One day afterwards, Fairweather, who said he couldn't read, had the CO and a couple of other pilots in his taxi plane. As usual, he brought out his cigarette case and passed it around. As he came to the astonished CO, Fairweather asked without batting an eyelash, "Would you care for an instant dismissal, sir?"

I have a few other memories of those days at Luton. On September 13, 1942, I took my first solo ride in an aircraft without a checkout – a 125-hp Tiger Moth trainer. It was the gentle beginning of the system of being able to fly strange planes without any previous instruction, which is one of the characteristics of an ATA pilot. I also had a checkout, dual, in a Fairchild 24, an American cabin plane which four months previous I would have considered a "big job." When I flew the Argus, as they called it, I thought of the $10 an hour I had spent one afternoon in California for the privilege of such a thrilling experience. Ten dollars an hour – and now I was being paid to fly it! How strange and wonderful!

My first actual delivery was a "Maggie" – and what fun! I kept tabs on every little road, back alley and tree so as not to get lost. The Maggie safely put away, I climbed into a big twin-engined Wellington bomber with Miss May and enjoyed my first "stooge" (passenger) ride with a female driver in such an aircraft. We often flew as stooges with other ATA pilots, which helped in delivering us to our next ferry job or back to base.

During the latter part of this period I purchased my uniform. That is, the ATA supplied it, but it took about three months after the measurements and fittings were taken to wear it in public. My, it was a proud day for that uniform! I was shaking so much that Mary N. had to tie my tie for me, and my side cap just wouldn't stay put. My very thin gold stripes, cadet officer, looked big enough to be commander stripes. I had no wings yet, not until I finished EFTS (Elementary Flying Training School).

When Commander Pickup called us into his office to tell us that we had completed the course, he didn't make any fancy presentations. He just said, "Be careful, especially taxiing. You are posted to White Waltham for advanced training, reporting tomorrow afternoon. Here are your chits [written orders] for your wings. You can draw [get] them at the store."

That was all. The little man in the store gave us a couple pairs of wings and congratulated us. There was no fancy parade, no "General Whoosis" pinning bright wings onto our pockets or flight leaders handing them out. It was just a routine matter, without a bit of fanfare – in keeping with ATA tradition.

Miss Cochran stayed until the last group arrived in August 1942. She had lived several years in England, although New York and Indio, California, were her homes. Upon returning, she became administrator of the WASP training. Just before she left, she gave a party in London for all us girls, and that gave me my first experience in a blackout with a torch (flashlight).

It was Sunday and I had flown late. I dashed around collecting my overnight gear and puffed uphill to the bus stop. Here I waited and waited. Finally, a man told me that there were no more buses to London. I groaned. However, with his and his wife's help, I managed to get to the railway station and catch a train – on which I stood for the hour's journey.

Arriving in London, I could see nothing. I followed someone else's torch downstairs onto a street. Here I was lost. I just stood. Finally, a man came up and asked me if I were lost, which was not even amusing. He led me across the dark street; stumbling off the curb, I caught a bus. I found my hotel, then walked to another hotel five blocks away for the party. It was so dark I had to ask my way several times and nearly fell off the curb at each intersection. I pulled up one fellow, and he answered with laughter in his voice, "Why, yes, this is Grosvenor House right here," and he had to lead me ten feet to the unlit entrance. I arrived at 10:00 PM, just as the party was breaking up. However, Miss Cochran took several of us to her London flat (apartment) and fed us.

After that experience I avoided going out in a blackout or fog except in an emergency – and always with a torch. Dim-outs, brownouts, and blackouts are heaven after a heavy London fog and not a peep of light showing. It's really indescribable – a sort of detached feeling, a groping through space. There is no shape or form to anything, and a torch in the fog doesn't help a bit. It's a continuous bumping into others, millions of muttered "'cuse me's," sliding one's feet off the curb in order not to fall, and wondering where the heck you are.

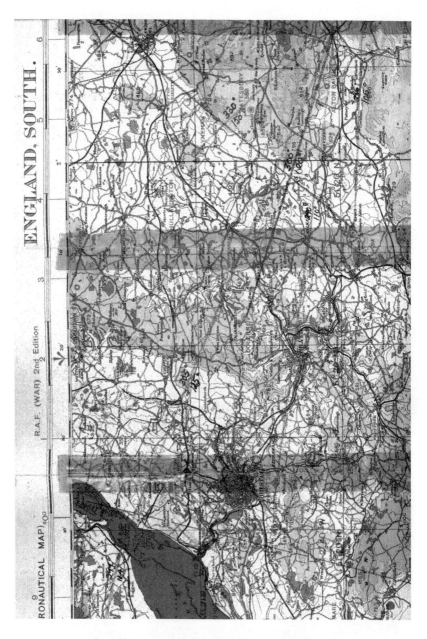

A well-worn map I carried flying in England

IV.

AND MAY I PRESENT _____ ?

It was at Luton that most of us first met the commandant of women pilots, Miss Pauline Gower, now Mrs. Fahie, daughter of an MP (member of parliament): middle 30's, blond, an aviation pioneer with several thousand hours who fought successfully for women ferry pilots. In January 1940, she recruited eight experienced (all with over 1,000 hours) women for trial in the ATA who were to prove that women could ferry any and every type of aircraft needed by the RAF or Fleet Air Arm (Naval Aviation). The original eight were Marian Wilberforce, Margaret Fairweather, Margaret Ebbage, Rosemary Rees, Winifred Crossley Fair, Joan Hughes, Mona Friedlander, and Gabrielle Patterson.

These women, supplemented by others in June and the following months, flew Tiger Moths and other light trainers for about a year before being allowed to fly faster planes. Then came the Miles Master (a trainer similar to the AT-6), Oxfords (light twin-engines), Hurricanes, Spitfires, and later, Blenheims, Wellingtons, Hudsons, and other twin-engine and fighter aircraft. In the spring of 1943,

Lettice Curtis became the first woman to fly a four-engine airplane, the Halifax, as pilot-in-command (PIC), and "solo" at that! Only a non-pilot flight engineer accompanied her, as was true in all her deliveries.

Due mainly to the inspiration and leadership of Miss Gower, plus the fine record of the pioneers, women became an integral part of the ATA. Eventually, there were two complete stations ("pools") out of 16 composed entirely of women, with women pilots at four other pools. They formed about one fifth of the total pilot personnel. Amy Johnson Mollison, one of the foremost British pilots, lost her life while in the ATA. Caught by bad weather over London, she bailed out, landing in the Thames River. As the story goes, she struggled to the rescue boat, but some part of the boat hit her and she drowned.

It was at Luton too that members of the American contingent began to know each other. Some of the first group mentioned to us the suspicion that the British women had about us. Most of them resented our presence because they figured we wouldn't last out our contracts, that we would go home as soon as we had some hard work, that we looked upon the job entirely as adventure and a lark, that we were paid more, and that it was only a means of gaining experience so we could get better jobs in America. Since most of us had a fair amount of experience, we shot ahead faster than some others, which upset them too. However, in the long run, we came to understand each other and there wasn't so much of that sort of antagonism. Some American men in the days of '40 and '41 had given a rather bad account of themselves, so it's said, and the British were not too sure of the women. However, I know a few people will miss us with all our cigarettes, candy, and the other odds and ends that we used to scrounge for them!

In the first group to arrive in March 1942 were Virginia Farr, Winnibelle Pierce, Louise Schuurman, Dorothy Bragg, and Helen Richey. Ginny had been an instructor in New York and New Jersey, her home state. Louise ("Dutchie"), youngest of the entire group of twenty four, had her first American citizenship papers. Her father was the Dutch consul-general in Chicago. Helen Richey was an old-timer with a good number of hours and years of experience. She had flown as a co-pilot on an airline and had done some teaching. Dorothy Bragg (Fury) of New Orleans married a young RAF pilot, but he was later killed in a raid over Germany. Winnie Pierce became well known as the motorcycle gal, as she ripped along on her iron steed. One night she failed to make a turn and spent several weeks sick leave with an injured head. Much more dangerous than flying!

American Women in the ATA, 1942-1945

(Names used during service with ATA are in bold)

American women recruited by Jackie Cochran:

Opal **Anderson** Averitt
Winnie **Pierce** Beasley
Myrtle (Mikki) **Allen** Carter
Emily **Chapin**
Peggy **Lennox** Drown
Virginia **Farr**
Sue **Humphries** Ford de Flores
Mary Zerbel **Hooper Ford**
Virginia **Garst**
Una **Goodwin**
Dorothy **Furey Bragg** Beatty Hewitt
Roberta **Sandoz Leveaux**
Evelyn **Hudson** Richards
Polly **Potter** Forsstrom Ross

Mary Webb **Nicholson**
Hazel **Raines**
Helen **Richey**
Nancy **Miller** Livingston Stratford
Edith Foltz **Stearns**
Grace **Stevenson**
Catherine **Van Doozer**
Ann **Wood** Kelly

Canadian:
Helen **Harrison** Bristol

Dutch:
Louise **Schuurman**

American women who joined the ATA on their own:
Aline **Rhonie** Brooks
Betty **Lussier**
Jane **Plant** Spencer

The second group, arriving in April, consisted of Hazel Raines of Georgia, Grace Stevenson of Oklahoma, Susanne Ford of New York, and Virginia Garst of Missouri. The last had an appendectomy just after arriving and, not making a rapid recovery, she returned home. Hazel, with her southern accent, shared the spotlight with Dorothy Bragg in amusing the British with her drawl. Hazel had a narrow escape in a Spitfire when the engine cut and she plowed through the top of a thatched-roof house. The aircraft disintegrated but Hazel, sitting in the strong cockpit, escaped with only a bad head cut and bruised knee. Grace went to Spartan School in Tulsa, Oklahoma, where she spent a year in the hangar and air to equip herself for flying as a career. She had instructed in several

CPT programs before joining the ATA. Aside from flying in the ATA, she seemed mostly involved in battling Anna Leska, Polish girl, in backgammon, bridge, or pontoon (blackjack). Sue Ford enjoyed flying at home more as a sport than as a profession.

Ann Wood, Polly Potter, and Helen Harrison comprised the third group. Ann- tall, brunette, pleasant- had the knack of being frank and honest in a nice way, so she became the diplomat of the whole contingent. Polly returned immediately to the States due to illness. Helen, a Canadian, had a good deal of experience and had taught flying for years, including in South Africa. One of her South African (British) pupils was Jackie Sorour, who had joined the ATA in 1941.

The largest number came in the fourth party, which arrived in June. Edith Stearns of Oregon was possibly the most experienced of the total group, having about 4,000 hours in fifteen years of flying. She had an interest in the first feeder airline in the United States; had flown as co-pilot on an airline; and had taught many pupils, including her 18-year-old son. At that time, she was the only mother to have soloed her son. Kay Van Doozer formed with Edith the "grandmother's club," being the eldest (although they were not very old) of the total group. Kay provided a great deal of good cheer and wit to keep us happy on those cold, wet washout days. There was also Peggy Lennox, a former instructor. She was keen on photography and took many pictures.

Evelyn Hudson, born in England, became a naturalized citizen of the States in order to instruct. I had seen her once near my home, but she was too busy with the CPT program to take outside students. She had lovely long hair done in a braid around her head, her main recognition point. She had some hard luck in 1943 when a Wellington bomber in which she was riding as a passenger crashed after takeoff. She spent six months in a Canadian hospital, mostly flat on her back recovering from crushed vertebrae. Her courage throughout the ordeal was remarkable, and her recovery was even more so. We used to visit her, and she always said we did so in order to eat her good lunch. She returned to the States and tried to return in October 1944, fully recovered, but Air Ministry refused to allow the ATA to sign any new contracts at that time.

Una Goodwin returned home after a few months due to illness. Mary Zerbel had taken her instructor's course from the same person as I had, Harry Ross, in Los Angeles. We had met each other a few times. Mary had tried to get into the ATA in 1941, as her fiancé was serving in the RAF Coastal Command in Britain. They were married soon after Mary arrived, but two months later to the day, he was reported missing and eventually killed in action. Two years later she married a US B-24 pilot, Jack Ford, and they returned to the States at the completion of his tour of operations.

The fifth group officially was only myself, since Opal Anderson had signed her contract with the previous group. Opal had been barnstorming and instructing for years and always provided lots of laughs with her good humor. The last group landed in August with three New Yorkers: Emily Chapin, Mary Nicholson (originally from North Carolina), Myrtle (Miki) Allen, and Roberta Sandoz of Washington. Bobbie had taken her check with me but contracted pneumonia and remained in Canada until the final group. Except for Mary, these were the most inexperienced pilots, with only 150-250 hours apiece. Bobbie was the third to marry but was different in that she chose a British Army captain rather than a pilot. We trained at different times and were stationed at various pools, so we really didn't know each other very well.

While most of the women (and men too) were British, the American contingents were the largest. About 200 American men participated, most of whom returned to the US when December 7, 1941, arrived. There were also women pilots from New Zealand (four), Australia (two), S. Africa and Poland (three each), Canada (five), and one each from Denmark, Holland, Argentina, and Chile.

About 31 different countries were represented in the ATA overall, men and women.

Most outstanding and unbelievable, we had men with handicaps that would ground most pilots. Charles Dutton was a tall, thin, lanky pilot. He usually flew single-engines and probably had more Spitfire deliveries than any other ATA pilot. That's not so remarkable though. What is amazing is that he only had one arm, the left one; the other had been amputated at the shoulder after a football accident in his youth. He had learned to fly with one arm and he continued into the ATA, flying all types of fast aircraft- Spits, Typhoons, Tempests, etc.

And he did it well too. He was very long-legged and long-armed, so he could use his legs to hold the stick while the left hand opened or closed the throttle. He made slight corrections with quick motions of his hand, and you must remember the hand is quicker than the eye. But I can't figure how he managed on some of the operations. The Spit landing gear lever is on the far right – which meant his long left arm had to reach completely across to use it. How he got along so well I guess nobody will ever know except himself.

Even stranger though was Corrie, who had a four-inch stump from his left shoulder and a normal right arm. He flew twin-engines as well as single-engines. Not only that, but he flew many Mosquitoes, which have the throttles on the left side. Keith Jopp was the third one-armed pilot in ATA. He was a WWI pilot, 50 years old, with one arm and one eye, yet he delivered aircraft until the end of the ATA in 1945. With a hook for a hand and know-how, he managed single-engines too.

Remarkable men. I suppose some people would say that they are dangerous pilots. However, they seem to have a lot better records than many two-handed pilots and have flown numerous types of aircraft safely.

Contact! Britain!

After finishing the cross-country tours to learn map reading, Opal and I were sent to White Waltham Aerodrome for advanced training. White Waltham (WW) was an hour's train journey west of London and allowed us time to pop into town. It was the headquarters of the ATA and therefore had many buildings, as well as many people with all sorts of gold braid on their shoulders. Ground school kept us occupied for three weeks, and then we flew as weather permitted- since it was October, that was only occasionally. I spent five months of winter at White Waltham, and the most pleasant part of the whole deal was when I was posted to 15 Ferry Pool, Hamble, near the famous port of Southampton, on March 6, 1943.

However, before then I made a marvelous discovery one night. For lack of hotel rooms in London, I finally called the Nurses' Club of the American Red Cross, where they gave me a bed. Mrs. J.A.D. Biddle, wife of the ambassador, heard about my plight- the impossibility of enjoying leave in London due to lack of accommodation. A week later she told me that all the American ATA girls could sleep at the Red Cross any time. This kindness was typical of the Red Cross organization everywhere in Britain.

I came down with flu at this club, so the cold injection shots which I took later were a bit tardy. Winter time always provided me with colds galore, caused by the terrific dampness. The nurses all popped into say hello and to do anything they could for me. They even gave me some grand peanuts from the Post Exchange, which were delicious. That is, they were until I ate too many. I had to get a doctor out of bed at midnight and at 4:00 AM to relieve my case of acute – and it was acute – indigestion. It's cause for no laughter; I have never doubled up in pain so much as I did then.

The club "grew up" as the months passed. We had real coca-colas for months, but they finally faded out and then we had colored fizz-water (officially called pepsi-cola). The snack bar was filled with an array of sandwiches, pastries, salads, coffee, milk shakes (without ice cream), and specialties. It was a lively room, the walls plastered with all sorts of odd posters and college pennants hanging from the ceiling. The club had movies, dances, fortune tellers, etc. on various nights. The American male officers, who were welcomed to all meals and entertainment, often played the piano or a strenuous game of ping-pong.

The best and most common game was a certain conversation beginning:

"What state do you hail from?" (Without regard for grammar)

"California"

"You are? What city?"

"Los Angeles"

"My golly! I have a friend there. Do you know _____?"

That would start it. Even if two people came from different sections of the country, there would be a "Do you know _____" conversation. And if someone did know whoosis, there would be great rejoicing and an animated five minutes of "Have you heard from him recently?" "What is she doing?" "Did you know his (or her) friend so-and-so?" Etc. etc. But if a person came from Florida or Texas (or any other state for that matter), friendly feuds began at once over the greatness of their respective states, providing an interesting and amusing sideshow for the others.

Contact! Britain!

V.

AND HERE WE HAVE THE
HURRICANE

Ground school was a dull period for most of us who wanted to fly immediately. However, we plugged along in our advanced training at WW that winter, learning about superchargers, carburetors, theory of flight, propeller systems, automatic boost, hydraulic system for the landing gear and flaps, icing, etc. The time came for the horrid written and oral examinations through which we all bluffed – and the instructors knew it. Then we started flying the AT-6 Harvard, and I wondered if I could fly it better here than in Montreal.

Fortunately, everything went along okay and I soon bounced along solo. After a couple of cross-country jaunts and runway landings, I hopped into a Master I, an English low-wing trainer. How Captain Joan Hughes, with all of her 5'2", managed to peer out of the back cockpit I don't know – she was certainly propped up with pillows. Then came the biggest moment in school: solo in the

Hawker Hurricane, one of the foremost British fighters. We jumped from 715 hp to 1,030 hp, with no dual, only a ground cockpit check.

It brings your heart right up into your throat to sit in the cockpit, knowing you cannot have any guiding hand to help. White Waltham is a rough grass airfield, and the Hurricane tends to pitch back and forth, so you can just imagine what sort of takeoff was usually made. Mine was even worse than I had imagined. I hit every ridge at the wrong oscillation of the "Hurry," and all I could do was to push the throttle forward and pull gently back on the stick. It was a horrible feeling of bumping and skidding across the ground to hit another bump, with my hand trying to keep the stick in a half-way decent position.

Finally, she lifted clear of the ground and stayed off. I shifted my left hand to the stick, my right to the undercart level at the right. Of course, the safety catch decided not to play fair, and I couldn't get the wheels up until I had climbed about 1,000 feet. But once in the air, it was an entirely different feeling from the trainers: the feel of power, the tug at the leash as if the Hurricane wanted to fly away on its own. The controls were light, except for the aileron, and it had to be "flown" because of the pitching instability.

After ten minutes, I could make fairly decent turns without my insides tightening up. The u-approach was quite fair, and the visibility on the left side of the cockpit was good. Somehow on this first landing, I missed all the ridges and bumps and put the machine down practically without feeling it touch. I made a couple more circuits and bumps, the takeoffs getting better (they couldn't be worse) and the bumps more bumpy, so I quit!

I believe that solo was one of the greatest thrills I've had. For most of the school students, it was the same. Hazel, Helen H., and Ginny considered it important enough to write a song about the great event. I shall repeat it here, and if you can swing out with the tune of "The Wreck of the Old 97," maybe you'll enjoy it too. For explanation, HTTMPPFG is a drill we had to learn (hydraulics, throttle tension, trim, mixture, etc.) "Temperature" refers to glycol (radiator) temperature. "Selector" is the landing gear lever. "Red light" shows that the gear is locked up. When the throttle is closed, "the horn" blows, indicating the gear is up or unlocked. The rest is self-explanatory. It is called "A Circuit in a Flurry and a Hurry."

She was taxiing down the field
    Doing 50 miles per hour
When the temperature began to rise
    HTTMPPFG
    In a hell of a hurry
And away she took to the skies.
When she reached the cruising level
    Still working like the devil
The selector would not go.
She was wet with perspiration
    From this awful situation
When the red lights began to show.
So she struggled round the circuit
    Pushing knobs, tabs, and levers
Mixture, flaps, pitch and gills did she do.
But the gear she forgot
    In the throes of her panic.
She had done the very best
    That she knew.
She descended in a glide
    Doing 90 miles per hour
When the horn began to blow.
She was found in the wreck
    With her hand on the throttle,
And she said,
    What a jolly good show!

Contact! Britain!

Jean Bird, who was living with me at the time, insisted that I celebrate my first Hurricane. We scooted down to Sunny's in her jalopy with the famous license number beginning "DFC." There we had dinner with Honore Salmon (British) and Hazel Raines (American). Insisting that I really celebrate, Jean spent all night and all her money trying to find a "hard" drink that I liked. I would take a sip or two of each, shake my head, put it down; Jean finished them. Eventually, I could barely throw darts at the board, and Jean just sat. We both slept well – and, remarkably, no hang-overs!

My favorite: the "Spitfire" fighter

Logbook pages, 1944

SUMMARY FOR: APRIL·1944
UNIT: 15 F.P.

Type	Time
HUDSON (1)	1:00
VENTURA (1)	0:50
BLENHEIM (1)	0:40
MOSQUITO (1)	0:45
ALBACORE (1)	0:10
SWORDFISH (2)	1:60
HURRICANE (1)	1:10
OXSTRIE (1)	0:15
FAIRCHILD (TAXI)	6:05
ANSON (1)	3:30
AVENGER (3)	3:6
SEA-OTTER (4)	3:05
SWIFTFIRE (9)	5:35
SEAFIRE (5)	2:35
WALRUS (2)	1:10
OXFORD (4)	5:35
BARRACUDA (2)	1:40
TYPHOON (5)	2:55
(18 TYPES) (49)	40:05

Caption: Quite an assortment of airplanes in a short time!

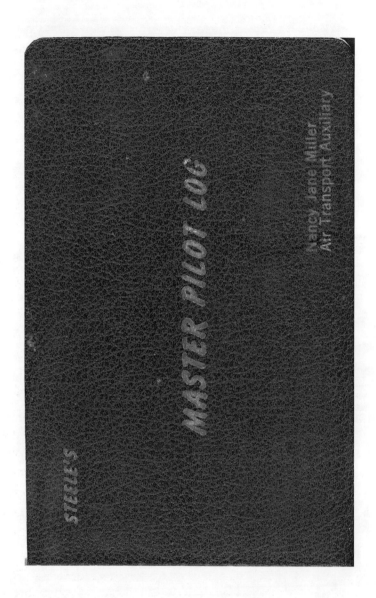

A logbook is a record of a pilot's life in the air. Here is the well-worn cover of mine.

VI.

MRS. ROOSEVELT DOES IT AGAIN

After the Hurricane solo, we came into the Training Pool, which served as a ferrying unit attached to headquarters, but under strict supervision. We learned what to do with our "chits" (orders for type of aircraft, from and to where, etc.), when we had to send signals, what to do in case of a forced landing, how to make out "snag sheets" (items requiring maintenance), etc. Aircraft were selected with care by the operations officer according to the experience of the pilot, and after a certain number of deliveries in various planes, we were posted permanently to one of the regular pools.

On January 9, 1943, I scooted up the coast in a Hurricane. The weather set in, and for three days I watched movies and griped about the terrible fog. Finally came a delightful day, and I set out in a Lysander (high-wing, very slow-stalling air-sea-rescue observation plane) for the Isle of Man. That little island is between England and Ireland with lots of water surrounding it. I was quite happy until I left the northern tip of Wales; then I felt the outline of the dingy on which I was sitting more definitely. I thought of the cold water below, of the Air-Sea Rescue squadrons that had saved hundreds of aircrew lives, and then I prayed that the "Lizzy" would keep running. The clouds got lower, and when I didn't see land after fifteen minutes as I had expected, I became a bit worried. My ETA was eighteen minutes. At sixteen and a half minutes, I saw the coastline—it was blurred by a slight haze, but nevertheless, my relief was indescribable.

I went into a small town and had two eggs for lunch, the first I had had in three months. Did they taste good! I bought six eggs, packed them well, and tied them securely to the back of the cockpit of the Gauntlet (a bi-plane similar to a Gladiator, still a front-line fighter in 1938, although really of vintage 1930). The Gauntlet, bless its heart, performed beautifully, and I crossed back to the mainland feeling absolutely on top of the world. I made one of the smoothest landings of my career—no scrambled eggs! When I think of the uneasiness fifteen minutes gave me over the water, I wonder what Lindbergh and some of the others thought and felt on their single-engine jaunts across the ocean!

Just before posting, we usually had one or two Spitfires to deliver, a sort of bonus for lasting through training pool. My first Spit was one of the oldest marks, with its logbook showing entries as far back as 1939, pre-Battle-of-Britain days. It was a great thrill to sail away at over 200 mph on that clear day of February 26, 1943. The controls were so light that only the slightest pressure was needed for maneuvering. There are a great many American lads who would have liked to have been in my place, I know! It was, and is, a great plane.

There were many washout ("scrubbed") days during Training Pool due to weather, and I remember Captain Head and his paper models. With thin pieces of cardboard, stiff note paper, and glue, he used to design special aircraft models for the amusement of himself and any onlookers. He would always test fly them to work out the kinks. We used to watch with bulging eyes as Captain Head, standing precariously on a chair or table, would launch his newest pet and see it dip to one side and crunch into the wall, or soar gracefully the length of the long room.

One day we saw DRO's (Daily Routine Orders) to the effect that a parade of some sort was imminent and all pilots must be in full dress. For us gals, that meant our skirts instead of slacks, black stockings, side caps, and keeping unruly hair above collars. Of course, the gossip strained the grapevine, and we figured that anyone from the King and Queen, Mr. Churchill, Mrs. Roosevelt (she was somewhere in England), or Sir Stafford Cripps was to visit us.

The day came, as many do, pouring rain. Aircraft lined the tarmac in front of the hangars, and several women were to stand in front of each one – since Mrs. Roosevelt, Mrs. Churchill, and Colonel (Mrs.) Hobby (the head of the US Women's Army Corps) were coming. Some of us had luck. The high Fairchild wing protected us until the last moment, when we stepped in front of the propeller to receive Mrs. Roosevelt. All I can remember was her pleasant smile, her apology for making us stand in the rain, and the big black umbrella held over her by an ATA fireman. As soon as she passed, we scooted for the hangar. The other girls, poor souls, were drenched to the skin, but none caught pneumonia.

Afterwards in the tea room, I shook hands with Mrs. Hobby, and the only thing I can recall was that I didn't like her stiff military hat. It was most interesting to talk with them all informally though.

It was more exciting, however, when the air raid siren sounded just after they left. We were all sure that the Germans had "inside information" about Mrs. Roosevelt and only the bad weather prevented possibly serious damage. Several bombs were dropped on a nearby airfield, evidently mistaken for White Waltham. It was the first time I had been in a shelter, and I didn't like it. Poor Miss Gower, soaking from her tour with Mrs. Roosevelt (she didn't have an umbrella), was caught having a hot bath and had to do some hurried dressing – just in time to hear the all-clear.

Dealing with VIPs

Commodore d'Erlanger was the big white chief of ATA. I only had two run-ins with him, both embarrassing. One day an order appeared that we must salute all high-ranking officers of the ATA and all forces. Not knowing how to salute, I practiced for a while. Later that day, attired in cap and all, I went into the flying control to book in after delivering my plane. To my horror I saw d'Erlanger inside. I was absolutely petrified. I entered, but my arms just wouldn't budge from my sides! He looked around at me, and I took up my taxi sheet and wrote on it furiously. He said, "Good afternoon" to which I replied, but still my hands kept a close grip on the pencil and paper. I'm sure he realized what had happened, because he had the slightest twinkle in his eyes.

Oh my, I thought, what if he reports me! I flew back to Hamble and sorrowfully told my tale to Miss Gore, who could hardly keep back her laughter. She decided that I had disgraced the whole of Hamble and that I should be Fairchild taxi pilot for a week- a severe punishment which, of course, was never carried out!

One day I took off from Hamble for a five-minute delivery to a nearby airfield. The ground crew asked me to "shoot them up," to which I replied that I would if the engine percolated okay. Just before takeoff an Anson landed, and then I shot off. Everything seemed okay, so I turned in from 800 feet and buzzed right over the parked Anson and the ground crew further up the field. I then delivered the aircraft and came back by car. Miss Gore called me in, and I suddenly didn't feel too well.

"Nancy," she started sternly, but with a twinkle in her eye, "I personally don't mind you buzzing, but I would like very much if you would **not** do it over the CO's head!" It seems that d'Erlanger had come in the visiting Anson, over which I passed at naught feet.

I had to write an official letter one day, about somebody signaling me to the wrong place. All letters began "I have the honor to report _____," and finished "I remain, sir, your obedient servant _____," both expressions strange to and disliked by me. I finally came to the ending of the letter but couldn't think of the proper final sentence. Fuming, I put down, "I remain, sir, your humble servant _____." When Captain Head saw it, he grinned and said, "Yes, the letter's okay, but you don't need to be humble about it."

My first Christmas away from home was a bit hard to take. I volunteered to fly that day in order to forget it as much as I could. Unfortunately, there was no flying, so I was released in time to enjoy a luscious turkey dinner at my billet. I invited Mary Zerbel Hooper, and afterwards we just sat in front of the fire and tried hard not to let our feelings get the better of us.

There were two things I missed mainly. First was the beautiful Christmas Eve service in my father's church. I loved the candle-light procession, the rich choir music, and the atmosphere associated with this important date in Christianity. Secondly, I missed the six-foot Christmas tree and the fun in decorating it. Mother and I always insisted on a tree despite the good-natured grumbling of Dad, who would break down at the last moment to buy us one. He enjoyed the tree as much as we did, but he would always blame us for having one.

Contact! Britain!

VII.

"POSTED"? – OH, YOU MEAN "STATIONED"

It was on March 6, 1943, that Hamble, 15 ferry pool, suffered my presence as a full-fledged second officer. This was the beginning of many pleasant memories which were to offset the long unhappy winter's months of training. The routine and atmosphere were changed, and I felt for the first time a sort of freedom and relaxation. Finally I was really able to contribute to the war effort.

Hamble was the outgrowth of the experiment with women pilots. It was at that time the only all-women's pool, even as to MT (motor transport) drivers, adjutant, met (weather forecaster – a WAAF or Women's Auxiliary Air Force), office staff, operation officers, CO. For a group of 50 to 60 women working together, it was an amazingly happy and efficient group. Its apparently lazy atmosphere was a boon to my definitely lazy attitude; yet when there was work to do, it was carried out as quickly and efficiently as could be done in the unpredictable aviation business.

Miss Margot Gore, Commanding Officer, was the tenth woman to join the ATA and had a natural knack for leadership which commanded respect. Pre-war she had done some private flying and taught a bit. She was secretary for a couple of large concerns and was in the War Office when the ATA was formed. In the latter part of 1943, she was awarded the British Empire Medal for her fine service in the ATA.

Rosemary Rees, second in command, and Connie Leathert, third, spoke quickly and in a sort of monotone, which made them hard to understand. Rose had been a ballet dancer pre-war, and every once in a while you would catch her with arms and legs flying wildly as she practiced her "limbering-up" exercises. Connie was one of the first licensed pilots in England, the 12th I believe, receiving it in 1927. Stocky Connie indulged mainly in backgammon feuds with Anna Leska and Faith Bennett. She had owned and operated several planes pre-war.

My old friends Jean Bird and Honore Salmon were at Hamble. There were a few who had made flying their career, such as Philippa Bennett and Jackie Sorour of South Africa. Faith Bennett, wife of Charles Bennett the Hollywood scenario writer, had been in London theaters and had lived in California a few years. Mary Fuller-Hall had been a typist, and Mary Wilkins owned a little shop. Jean, Jackie, and Dora Lang all had transferred from the British WAAF to the ATA. Pat Parker, the first woman flight engineer, had been a school teacher.

Many of the women had only 10 to 50 hours flying when they joined ATA, for the sport was very expensive in pre-war England. Now, with 400 to 600 hours, they fly all sorts of single-engine fighters and twin-engine bombers. It is a tribute to all these British women that they had the stuff to stick the game through despite their relative inexperience and the unfortunate prejudice of the public against them.

The Making of a Pilot

I was not like others who started flying early, or who had a family upbringing in planes, or who worked around airports. My first airplane ride came because my brother Dick offered me a choice of a ride in the Goodyear blimp or an airplane as his 16th birthday present to me. We went out to the Grand Central Airport in Burbank, which is no longer there but was close by the present Burbank Airport in the valley north of Los Angeles. The ride was for about half an hour over Los Angeles.

Dick and I sat in the back of a Stinson Reliant, as I recall. I realized later that an advanced student was flying the plane, with the instructor in the right seat—the way students used to gain time for their certificates. He took off, flew around LA, and made gentle turns. It was interesting to look down on the area, which was much clearer back in the mid-1930s. Everything looked so small, and you could see so far. But there was practically no sensation of movement, although Dick tried to right the plane by leaning "upwards" every time a gentle bank was made!

Although I was enjoying it, I was unimpressed—that is, until the final approach. Coming in a little high, the pilot entered what I learned later was called a "slip." He eased the nose to the right and lowered his left wing, maintaining a straight direction to the runway. The plane shuddered a bit (all older pilots remember the sensation) and dropped rather steeply, to lose altitude. I was on the left, down-wing side, and suddenly I was grabbed by a wonderful feeling of motion and wonder at the plane's steep descent. I gave out a whoop of joy. Dick, bless his heart, was grabbing the upper part of the plane wherever he could but kept sliding down onto me as far as the seat belts would allow. As the plane straightened out and landed, I thought, "At least the last part was great fun." Dick did not feel exactly the same way!

Afterwards, as I described our experience to my father, he just smiled. He knew I might ask him if I could take some flying lessons, and he had his answer and his reasons ready. They were sensible to him, and somewhat to me, but I was disappointed of course. It was another case of a teenager being suddenly excited about something and wanting to do it – and then being deflated and returning to other activities.

Prior to flying, my interest had been in auto racing—why I'm not sure, except that my brother Randolph used to go to the old Ascot Raceway in the LA area, and he used to let his little 9- to 10-year-old sister tag along. I kept track of all the races, had my favorites, and I enjoyed the close races, the skidding turns, and the smell of the castor oil used then. I was also interested in sports generally, played on the GAA (Girls Athletic Association) school teams (swimming, baseball, field hockey).

I also participated in the neighborhood touch football games until I was about 15. Yes, I was the only girl, but a friend of my brother Dick always saw that I was "chosen" on a team and got to catch a ball or two. It was tremendous fun for me. Dick practiced boxing, bobbing and weaving and slapping an old punching bag back and forth. I recall him being on his knees and letting me, standing tall at six or seven years of age, try to hit him. I flailed away, and he used his quickness to avoid any hits. I grew so exasperated that I would begin to cry. Later, as I grew up, he taught me the rudiments of boxing- jabs and hooks- and we used to spar away, he always being the quicker. When I was 16, I happened to hit him on the nose, and it started to bleed. It was about the only time I had hit him in the head. Nothing serious, but I immediately retired as "champion"!

I didn't read much about the exploits of women pilots, although I did admire Amelia Earhart for forging ahead to do as the men had done in aviation. Her disappearance in 1937 saddened me, and I kept a large picture of her in a scrapbook, which I still have. In a sense I think her desire, as a woman, to fly as other men and women had – and more – possibly planted the seed in me to want to fly. However, there was no chance at the time: I was too young and had no support from the family.

So the seed was dormant until 1939. After two years at Occidental College in Los Angeles, I transferred to the University of California at Berkeley. There I noticed an article about the Civilian Pilot Training Program to be given by the government to some 110 boys and 10 girls. It consisted of 50 hours of ground school, given on Saturday mornings, and 35 hours of flight time during the week, leading up to a private license. Since World War II was already underway, with England being bombed by Germany, our government wanted to have some trained men pilots in reserve if or when the USA would be involved. But at first it was a "civilian" course and included some women, probably so as not to alarm the populace generally.

I asked for information, filled out an application, and then had to get my dad to sign a release and approval form, as I was under age at the time. He wrote back a letter listing all the reasons why he didn't think I should take the course (the primary one was because my mother was an invalid), but he signed the authorization form. I dropped the letter, raced to the office with the form, and was one of the 10 women accepted. I started training in December 1939 at the West Moreau Flying Service at the Oakland Airport.

Since this meant flying three times a week, usually beginning about 3:30 PM or later, along with the usual academic courses, it meant the latter did not receive all the attention that they should have. My grades went down, much to my parents' disapproval. But the desire for flying had been instilled in me, and my aviation studies became my first priority. I did not want to fail. It did not come easily, and I had to and did study hard.

Margot Duhalde, or Chile as we always called her, learned to fly in her native land. She became involved in some deal in which she was to fly for the French government, but France fell and she was stranded in England without knowing a single word of English. On entering the ATA, she was soon dismissed because she could not understand any instructions. Not deterred in the least, she studied English and worked as a ground engineer in order to pick up aeronautical terms. Finally she was re-admitted to the flying section and progressed rapidly. Often she provided great amusement with her accent and vocabulary, but she got even by jabbering away in Spanish with Maureen Dunlop, an English girl born in Argentina.

Ida Van Zanten was a quiet Dutch girl who had escaped from the Germans via a secret underground, traveling through Switzerland, France, Spain, Portugal, and finally to England. She told of several escape attempts by boat at night which were discovered by the German patrols and how they escaped by scampering through the dark fields.

Vera Strodl was a 5'8" Danish blond Viking, thoroughly interested in flying, bicycling, ice skating, horseback riding, fruits, and vegetables. She wore no makeup, but her natural healthy red cheeks, perfect set of white teeth, and ready smile were far more cheerful than artificial coloring. She was terribly keen on flying, and it was this great zeal that gave her the tremendous energy for meeting all obstacles in her path.

Vera was fifteen when she left Denmark. She had wanted to fly, but everyone discouraged her. She secured a job at the docks as an interpreter in order to earn enough money to go to England. Her experiments in flying included a jump off the barn roof with an umbrella and slipping down a cable pulley between two trees! When in England, she upped her age by two years to get a job as a dishwasher, then as a counter waitress.

She became an inspector in Phillip and Miles aircraft factory, earning £1 ($4-5) per week. From this she paid her room and board, eating mainly raw vegetables; paid insurance; and, at 18 years, had enough money saved to get her "A" (solo) license. She went into the Gloucester Aircraft plant and demanded £3-15-0 per week ($11). She was soon at the head of the inspecting job, with many working under her. It was a thrill a few years later to find herself in one of the P. and M.'s trainers with her own inspection plates everywhere on the plane!

During this time she kept flying as much as she could and took up gliding. She won her A and B licenses on the same day and her C later. She had one accident when the towing cable broke. The glider broke too, but Vera escaped injury. It was sad financially, however, as she had to pay the £25 ($100) insurance on it. With her wanderlust, she wanted to go to Australia. Everything was set for September 4, 1939, but late in August the trip was canceled. She then got a position testing Taylorcraft Austers. The job branched from three days into two years, but her position was always considered "temporary." When the requirements in the ATA were lowered, she entered the ferry service.

Our building at Hamble was just a one-story brick affair with one big lounge, a mess, a locker room, and a few offices. Later on, it expanded to include a pleasant sick quarters (especially for those with flu) and other offices. It was not a Nissen hut or a flimsy dirty building like many I've seen. Luckily, as I've remarked before, we did not have barracks in which to live but were billeted out to private families.

At first, though, I lived in a hotel where I met one lady who had a part-time war job. It was sorting various types of rivets. One of the aircraft factories had someone sweep up the rivets, put them through a "strainer," so to speak, in order to separate them from other materials and muck. Then these rivets were put into small bags and given to various women who volunteered. These people sorted them as to color, size, and shape and returned them in separate boxes for a final check and chemical washing. Thus the factories regained millions of what would have been wasted or useless rivets.

I moved into a small house with Mr. and Mrs. Whitcombe and their two sons, Mervin, 5, and Peter, 10. Mrs. Whitcombe spoiled me entirely by being an excellent cook, doing my washing, filling my hot water bottle at night, and feeding me real eggs. I had a small bedroom filled by a hard double bed and also a small sitting room. Everything was in blue, my favorite color.

Each morning at 8:35, I would be called in a high undulating boy's voice (like an air-raid siren), "Miss Miller, your breakfast is ready." Sometimes the boys would have a quarrel over the morning's privilege. Every morning when I came downstairs to go to work, Mervin would bounce through their door with a charming "Good morning, Miss Miller." It was such a ritual that I really didn't feel as if the day had started correctly unless I had my greetings – and Mervin only missed when sick or when he overslept.

Here I found that with good planning, there could be very good, well-balanced meals. The only food I missed was salad, especially a good hard chunk of lettuce with French dressing. Vegetables were scarce, potatoes and bread "standard equipment" to fill up the tummy. Meat and "sweets" (desserts) could be listed on one hand, but curiously enough they didn't become too monotonous. I had lunch at various airfields (sometimes not at all), and the American Red Cross food sufficed when "on leave" (furlough), so that some variety was introduced. Sometimes we'd really be lucky and be able to drop in at an American station, where the GI cooks would bring out the luxuries of peanut butter, jams, canned corn, fruits, fruit juices, etc.

The first five weeks at Hamble kept me busy mainly as the chief Fairchild taxi pilot- that is, collecting and delivering pilots in the plane. On "off" days, I flew lots of Spitfires, which was fun. Outside life was practically nil. One day I had the awful experience of flying my CO, which upset me greatly. I gave myself 75 percent, one slightly wheel landing, one good three-pointer. Either I scared her to death or she wanted to get rid of me, for the next week I was sent back to White Waltham for conversion onto twin-engines. On April 15th I had my first solo in the Oxford, powered by two 350-hp engines.

During the conversion I found time to sprain my ankle. I was running wildly to catch the ATA bus when my foot slipped over a drainage indentation. I missed the bus. The doctor sent me to the Canadian hospital for an x-ray, which was negative, and treatment, which was most unusual. After ascertaining through the x-rays that there were no breaks and figuring which ligaments were strained, he sprayed some stuff on it that froze all feeling. Then he ordered me to walk on it normally, then run or trot normally. I objected. However, I couldn't feel any pain, although it was swollen up twice its size. He ordered me to walk on it without limping as much as I could and have it sprayed once the next day and the following day. Except for slight pain for a couple days and a tendency to limp, I got along beautifully and in a week forgot about it. Quite different from the usual tape-winding medico with orders to use crutches. Peggy Lennox sprained her ankle and broke a small bone, necessitating a cast up to her knee. However, this didn't keep her from flying, and many a ground crew suffered a shock when Peggy hopped out of a Spitfire with a nice white anchor on her leg.

After my class 3 (Oxford) conversion, I went back to Hamble. During May I had an amusing experience while waiting for Anna to deliver a plane. I saw several Piper Cubs on the field and conveyed a strong hint that I should like to fly one again. By hook and crook, a lieutenant took me up. My goodness, I had a time! My coordination was nil, and I was terribly rough on the controls. Away we sailed bumpity bump and up we climbed as slow as molasses. I forgot the little engine only had 65 hp. We "sort of did" chandelles and lazy-eights, then a spin. Thinking of heavier aircraft, I shoved hard forward on the stick, and we both nearly went out of the top!

Then, after a few minutes of hedge-hopping, I approached to land. Everything was fine except that I couldn't believe the low speed of approach, and when I leveled off to land, I simply didn't have the strength of leverage to bring back the stick. Away came my hand from the throttle, and with both hands on the stick, giving a terrific tug, I managed to get the plane down okay.

I have so often heard of the big-plane pilots saying that they don't trust Cubs any more – so flimsy, slow, and only one engine. But most of them won't have enough money to fly anything else after the war, and then maybe they will get off their high horse and learn to fly one properly. We all will have to practice quite a few hours to regain our precision. It's amazing how much you must **fly** one of these grasshoppers.

On June 21st I flew my first P-51 Mustang, one of the finest American machines in the world (built according to British specifications). I used to watch them take off from the North American plant in Inglewood, California, without an inkling that I would fly one. But here it was. So pleased was I that I forgot safety in height. These Mustangs had a reputation for low-level attacks, so down to 50 feet I dove and hopped over trees and telegraph wires at 250-275 mph. Things rushed past in a blur, and there was certainly the sensation of speed.

As a finale, I shot across the airfield at 10 feet at just over 300 mph. Perhaps if you think of riding in a fast car, looking directly at the ground within a few feet of the tires, you have an idea of the blur. The sensation diminishes with height, and even at 100 feet, it only feels like riding in a car doing about 40 mph. At 1,000 feet, there is no sensation whatsoever. In approaching and landing, the angle of the earth seems suddenly to change from 50 feet downwards. There are various impressions involved, and that is why circuits and bumps are so interesting, especially the bumps!

On June 10th, while on leave in London, a friend called me and asked if I should like to broadcast to the States. Naturally I was jubilant. I traipsed off to the site of the event – the famous Rainbow corner, the American Red Cross Club off Piccadilly Circus – to have a preliminary interview with the lieutenant in charge. Then downstairs to the big room, the canteen, where a crowd of American enlisted men filled all the corners. They were everywhere! There were seven boys and myself to speak, with an interlude by a swing orchestra.

I was so busy pepping up the nervous fellow on my right that I managed to talk my two minutes okay. The lieutenant asked a few questions and I answered ad lib – no set script. As my stripe and a half on my shoulder gave me an equivalent rank of first lieutenant, this information brought hoots of derision from the privates, corporals, and sergeants. Also, the interviewer decided I should marry him and earn the family income flying while he did the dishes! The happiest thought was that this program was to be broadcast on the 12th in the States, which was my 24th birthday. We were allowed to send one cable home, which my father received, and it was a grand birthday present to myself, knowing that my family and friends would hear me then.

Amongst other things that England gave me was hay fever. For two months, May and June in each of my three years, my nose was like a leaky water faucet from springtime pollen. Every once in a while it became embarrassing, such as when I sneezed just as I was landing. Mostly it was just annoying. It seemed such a shame not to be able to enjoy the spring and the flowers! I kept quiet about it, as a severe hay fever or asthma was a "medical discharge" item.

I believe one thing that people underrate, although it has been publicized a great deal, is correspondence and packages to troops or anyone overseas. Mail was irregular due to submarine activity, roundabout routes, understaffed offices, lack of space. My letters came through the regular channels and the British system, not according to V-mail or the American APO. They usually arrived in bunches about every two weeks, taking four to six weeks for delivery. A fast trip was ten days.

Packages provided a form of subsistence, containing clothes unavailable in England or foods also not obtainable or with high coupon values. Hair grips (bobby pins), good quality lipsticks, rouge, hair nets, emery boards, chewing gum, peanuts, popcorn, olives, canned or dried fruits, fruit juices, soup mixtures, pudding mixtures ("add only water"), socks, stockings, shirts, ties (uniform necessity) – all were extremely welcome and invaluable. You could get along in Britain, but a parcel every two months sure brought wide smiles.

American magazines helped tremendously too. There were few good British ones due to paper shortages. My parents subscribed to *American, Cosmopolitan, Reader's Digest, Flying,* and *Air Facts.* The first two supplied the demand for short fiction and articles of American opinion. The last two kept me up with the flying front. The American *Reader's Digest* I have always liked, but instead of sending it across, the magazine sent the copy to the English office, where it was reprinted. Due to the paper shortage and a certain amount of censorship, many good cartoons and articles were omitted. The August English version would be just a three-quarters issue of the American June edition. I have seen American issues in the Red Cross and then two months later received the English version with omissions, poorer quality paper, and slightly smaller size.

My magazines were very popular with my British friends, and I dared not let them out of my sight until I had completely finished with them. Of course, the beautiful food advertisements fascinated them, as the English have never advertised so brilliantly, and the food looked so appetizing but was so unobtainable!

As to censorship, there certainly must have been a reason for it, but sometimes I wondered. Working in aviation, naturally we saw and flew many planes that were on the so-called "secret" list. We had to be careful in our talk and correspondence. My friends were compelled to address my letters (before V-E day) to the headquarters at Maidenhead, despite where I was stationed, but the British could write directly to my "pool." Then there was the time I wrote on ATA stationery. This was cut off by the censor (it was headquarters address), but my return address, exactly the same one, on the envelope was left intact. One wonders!

I received several letters from an ensign in America whose official address was the "USS YMS 93." One letter arrived with little holes chopped in it. It was obvious that every single hole had contained the number "93" referring to his ship. However, the return address on the envelope had not been touched.

One could buy maps all over England, detailed road maps. Spies could easily have them too, but nobody was allowed to send any home. The same with several books. One of the USA gals going home on leave in 1943 tried to take along a small book about the RAF with many pictures in it and signed by pilot friends in England. Although it was published in England, sold to anybody, and didn't contain the latest data, she could not take it with her. In America they published new books giving the same information, but still she could not carry it home. Guess it was too much for the censor to look on every page for a secret, invisible code!

The postmasters back home could not accept any sort of perishables for shipment to England. After all, the shipment took four to six weeks to arrive; thus fresh fruits, soft candies, etc. would have been likely to rot That was true up to a certain point. Soft candies like caramels, fudge, and Milky Ways could be sent and would arrive in good condition if they were well wrapped with wax paper. I received a box containing two long bars of delicious home-made chocolate fudge after a two months journey from California. I didn't eat the last bit until three months later (believe it or not), and except for being slightly stiff, it was still rich, creamy, and not stale. All candies will get somewhat stiff on a long journey, but if well wrapped, they will outlast any English sweets. And even if slightly stale, they were much better than war-time English candies.

Also, some censors would take advantage of parcels, as we all know. Some could not resist trying out some candies, chewing gum, cigarettes, or stockings. Of course, they did not use their censorship stamp or number on such parcels, so there could be no check up. It does make one furious at the petty dishonesties of persons in such responsible positions.

There was little to do around Hamble. We had six days off a month during the summer, four days in winter. It was necessary to have that rest from flying. Some would go to their homes, others visited friends, others went to London, others just loafed around the neighborhood. We could go into Southampton for a movie or take a dip in the Admiral's pool. This 2 x 4 bathtub provided cleaner exercise than in the river. In the summer Philippa tried her sailboat; she could not forget the possible £50 fine for civilians who were out on the bay, so she didn't do much of it. One day several of the American girls, including me, had the bright idea of playing baseball, much to the amusement and fright of the English gals. With a red tennis ball, a plank of wood for a bat, and bricks for bases, we let out howls, and the game was on. That was the first and last time, because we all wore ourselves out.

There were the tennis courts, usually "U/S" (unserviceable), ping pong tables, and a squash court on the field. There was a rifle range used by the home guard, but a team was formed by five pilots under the direction of the home-guard sergeant, and matches were arranged by mail. The most popular recreation seemed to be contract bridge. Backgammon was played often too.

Other items of interest around the airfield consisted of the local pubs; the local dances; and "Whiskey," "Tuppence," and "Bridget." The last two were cute little cocker spaniels bought by Kay V.D. What mischievous pups they were! Their lively attitude, as they grew, consisted of friendly knockout blows against all comers. They often wandered out to the ack-ack batteries and became fast friends with the gunnery boys. "Whiskey," the old Scottish terrier, just didn't know quite what to make of the other two at first – probably thought that an invasion had come. Eventually the two pups were separated, and we could travel around the neighborhood without fear of a good-natured attack!

The local pubs were the Yacht Club and the Bugle by the river. These were small hotels with a bar downstairs at which nearly everyone congregated to exchange gossip over some whisky, gin, or beer. Pubs are a special form of British life. People refer to them as landmarks and with a reverence that we Americans give to soda fountains. Often a person will give you directions and tell you to turn the next street past the "White Horse." Or perhaps they ask you first, "Do you know the "King's Arms?" and if you do, they give instructions from that pub.

Every pub is individual, much more so than our soda fountains. There may be one or two or more in each block, but with separate "individualities." Every one has a special atmosphere, due to the decorations, history, barmen or barmaids, and the people who frequent it. They are freer and friendlier than American bars. Men and women, old and young, make them a habit each day or night. Nearly every pub is crowded, full of smoke, yet there is a friendliness that holds people there. Often there are dart boards on the walls, and the games continue through the evening, through the smoke, and through the drinks. It is an easy-going, pleasant sort of past-time.

The principal drink is beer. Gin and scotch and others are not easily obtained. But there is nothing that quite compares to the Englishman with working clothes, sport or bowler hat, and huge walrus moustache when he expertly manipulates a foaming jug of beer to his mouth. Either he does it without disturbing a hair of that prize accumulation, or he whips off the foam from his moustache with a magnificent sweeping gesture!

The term "pub" refers to a building as well as to the actual bar. The pub usually is a very small hotel, for perhaps 10-50 guests, and a special room for drinking that can be entered either from the inside or outside. From the whole village, at around 8 PM the people congregate in the special room for a drink and to exchange the day's gossip and opinions. It is a form of entertainment and relaxation, for there is usually very little else to do in the evenings, so it has become an integral part of British life.

Down in the south, rather amazingly close to France, we had quite a few alerts. However, as with most things, one gets used to them, and I found myself sleeping through most of them. The Whitcombes had a sturdy little shelter behind the garage where, in 1940 during the real blitzes, they all slept. After the danger had passed, they moved back into the house. I went there for ten minutes one day when a single raider dropped a bomb about ten miles away. The second time was 7:30 Sunday morning when gunfire unmercifully woke me from my slumbers. I threw on my greatcoat (overcoat) and stumbled downstairs. When I was fully awake, I peered out of the shelter but saw nothing. Later, I found out that a German Junkers bomber had been overhead at 4,000 feet. I cursed him for waking me up, indiscriminate bombing (which did no harm), and for not letting me see him – safely!

These alerts seldom bothered me except when the river whistles blew, indicating "enemy within ten miles, heading this direction." This concerned me more, but still not as much as being in London with the Hyde Park rocket guns going full blast. There's something akin to claustrophobia in London, and the guns make an absolute hell of a row. Your heart thumps much faster, and it is difficult to maintain a steady walk or conversation.

Some people like London very much. I have never seen very much of it. Usually when I went on leave, I liked to relax, so I popped into the Nurses' Club, took in a few movies in Leicester Square, saw a few shows, etc. Restaurants don't have good food unless it is a special one, and then you must book a day or two in advance. The American Red Cross Clubs usually have good food at decent prices.

In these clubs you met so many people from America that you saw a cross-section of the States- their whims, opinions, likes and dislikes, temperaments, jokes, and prejudices. It is amazing to see the boys come and go. Most of the time you never know their names but play a game of ping pong or guzzle a coke with them. Maybe you see them again, maybe not. There are some of the old standbys who work in London. There are those on their first leave in London who are puzzled because they can't find anything to amuse themselves with. There are those who come in about once a month, and when they don't, you inquire from some of their friends. In March of 1944, I knew Lyle should be coming in, but he didn't show up. A letter I wrote him later was returned with "missing" on it. It was a sad time.

On a different note, I recollect one priceless moment at a railroad station when a GI, slightly tipsy, staggered up near me, saw the "USA" on my shoulder and asked excitedly,

"USA? What does that mean, lady?"

"Union South Africa," I answered with a sort of jerky accent. The way his face changed was so amusing. He shook his head, muttering "Wrong country. Wrong gal," and stumbled off

The winter of 1943 approached, and the days passed monotonously. Up at 7:45, dressed by 8:15 in front of an electric fire which did little to offset the penetrating cold. Mervin or Peter would call "Miss Miller, your breakfast is ready" in a high-pitched voice. After eating toast and tea, I'd slouch down the curved road to the legal entrance through the fence. Passing the hangars, I would stick out my neck far enough to see how the local skies appeared and then continue by "instruments" to the ATA building. Sometimes I'd glance at the thermometer to see just how cold it was. During the winter, the weather was usually foul. In summertime, it was almost as bad. The weather minima for the ATA were about equivalent to our American instrument minima. One day I recall it read 32 degrees F, just freezing. The next day, at precisely the same time, (9:00 AM), it read 52 degrees, a difference of 20 degrees. That is for people who don't believe the daily variation of British weather.

British Weather

The three song-writers, Peggy, Ginny, and Hazel, dedicated a song to the weather office or meteorological office at their station, Ratcliffe. In explanation, the Foss-way was a fairly straight Roman road used as a landmark, especially in bad weather. The tune is "You Are My Sunshine."

Where is that sunshine
My only sunshine
The met, he said it would be grand.
The vis was measured in terms of inches,
And the cloud base was touching the land.

So off I started
Right down the Foss-Way.
The route for all who travel south.
But all I know of that noted landmark,
Is what I've read in books and heard by word of mouth.

I saw no sunshine
I saw no Foss-way
How I arrived, I'll never know
One thing for certain, when leaving Ratcliffe
Catch up on all your prayers before you ever go.
AMEN!!!

Wandering down the corridor, I would look hopefully into my little "peephole" for mail. As mine usually came in bunches, there were many days when the box was empty. There were two spells of two months each when I received no letters from the States- quite upsetting. As I said, mail is one of the greatest morale boosters.

After the mail, I would enter the locker room to hang up my coat, hat, scarf, and gloves in my large wooden locker. I often muttered something about re-arranging my locker so that I'd have some space for things.

Then I'd pop into the "met" (weather) office. On one blackboard would be the day's forecast of cloud base, amount of cloud visibility, wind direction and strength, icing index, general notes, and any warnings. On the forecaster's desk would be the two early-morning charts showing the structure of the weather and its probable results, with a verbal explanation by the WAAF met forecaster. On another blackboard would be the actual hourly report of cloud, visibility, and wind from many stations throughout the country. These would give an indication whether to start writing letters, sew, play bridge, or just read the newspapers in anticipation of a job.

Pushing into the mess or main room, I could glance through a paper, usually the *Daily Express*, because it was flashier like the American papers, or the *Daily Mail* for "Archidamus" to see what my fortune was for the day, or the *Daily Mirror* for "Jane," the most famous comic strip in Britain. The latter character usually became involved with spies and often was caught half dressed. The newspapers had only four to six pages, in contrast to the thirty-six or more in American publications.

By 9:30, all the girls would straggle in, usually showing little life. By 9:45, either chits were out or a bridge game was on. At Hamble usually these chits were placed on a table, and there would be a crowding mass of humanity to see who had what. Upon the break of dawn, there would be mutterings of:

1) "Oh heck" [or worse], a Swordfish," meaning a very cold, slow trip in an open biplane.

2) "Drat it, taxi pilot," meaning jumping around in a Fairchild 24 or Anson to deliver and pick up pilots.

3) "Good show. A couple of connecting Spits," meaning not two attached Spitfires but a Spitfire from A to B and another from B to C, C being near home. Or,

4) "Cripes! A Beaufighter! I haven't even read the notes on it," meaning a dash to procure the white handling notes to prepare for a new type. And so forth.

The broadcast would be for "taxies and cars off at 10," which meant the taxi planes and cars which take the pilots to nearby airfields would start at that time. In other words, it meant checking up on the weather again for your particular route, a check on maps and overnight bag, a check of balloons and other obstructions over the route, a struggle into overalls and flying boots, a last-minute trip to the bathroom, and then trudging out with a parachute to the respective modes of transportation.

Balloons

I really think one of the most eerie feelings of war-time flying in England was taking off an airfield surrounded by balloons. In all innocence, one day when the weather was good everywhere but right at this factory, I took a chance. There were special lanes free of balloons, and I took off in lane "C" for "Charlie." The visibility and ceiling were so poor, though, that I couldn't see the balloons up at a thousand feet, and on the ground, I could just barely make out the cables – extending up into nothing. I couldn't even be sure that the lane was clear. But I blithely and foolishly climbed into my

Hurricane, rumbled off the rough grass airfield, and held my course on the directional gyro for two minutes before turning toward clearer weather to the west. I was lucky that time. However, after thinking about it, I never repeated the performance. Two other pilots were not so lucky. They hit the cables, damaging their wing tips, but fortunately they were able to land okay.

Even during good weather it is a peculiar feeling to come in between those balloons. One day I just started taxiing down to the takeoff point when the air-raid siren sounded, and as I looked up I saw the balloon popping up smack in the middle of the lane. They didn't waste any time. I had to wait on the ground until the "all clear." That in itself was a nervous time and brought on a thumping heartbeat. I felt like a sitting duck there, hoping no German plane would get through to strafe a lone aircraft out in the open. Or - more probably - hoping that no bombs would be dropped on the factory and field. Luckily, all went well.

At the collection place (factory, maintenance unit or MU, squadron, etc.), I would hand in my chit authorizing the collecting of the aircraft. This chit, by the way, consisted of four attached sheets. The top sheet you gave to the consignor; the second you had signed at the completion of the trip and took back to the pool as receipt for the delivery; the third was a signal form to be sent to a central headquarters to let them know the whereabouts of the plane; and a fourth sheet, given to the consignee, a snag sheet on which were written any faults noted on the delivery flight.

Snag Sheets

There are those who don't read snag sheets, which are to alert the engineer to fix any faults prior to the following flight.

One day I brought a very, very ropey Mosquito to its destination. It was a Mark III, a trainer with dual controls. The plane itself was old and beaten up; the petrol consumption of the starboard engine was about twice what it should have been; it was difficult to synchronize the engines, since you had to make continuous minor adjustments of pitch and throttle; and the port engine was idling about 900 rpm, while the starboard was okay at 600. I noticed it when I taxied out, for it was difficult to taxi, but I thought it would clear itself. I watched the engines carefully, made a takeoff okay, and eventually arrived at my destination. I checked my idling in the air by pulling both throttles full back, noticing that they were still 900 and 600. I upped the starboard to 900, made a fast landing, slowed down less quickly than usual, and braked very carefully. It handled quite all right. I put all the snags on the proper sheet and turned it into the engineer. I remarked verbally what a ropey old ship she was.

Two days later I had a call from the chief engineer – or somebody asking me about the Mossie delivery – if I had noticed anything wrong with the undercarriage. I said "No, my takeoff and landings were both okay."

"But you did say, on your arrival, that it was a particularly ropey aircraft."

"I certainly did," I answered emphatically. "In fact, it had three good snags which I put on the snag sheet."

"Oh, you did," in a surprised tone. "Can you tell just what these were?"

"Yes, I have my receipt in my file. If you wait a moment, I'll ask Captain Cook if I may have it." So I got the receipt and read the three snags. When I came to the last one about the rpm differences, he just said "Oh," as if that explained everything.

"Just what is this all about?" I asked, having a pretty good idea.

"Well, it seems that one of our pilots took it up and, coming in for a landing, he ground-looped and washed out the undercart. Didn't hurt himself, but of course the plane was a complete washout."

"I gave the engineer that snag sheet with a verbal warning. I couldn't have done more."

The chief something-or-other agreed with me and thought that the rpm variance was probably the cause of the trouble. I began to wonder what sort of pilots they had who wouldn't check their idling while running up or before taking off, and certainly the pilot should have noticed something peculiar during taxiing. And what sort of engineer wouldn't check snags! And then the pilot was trying to blame it on a previous undercart strain!

After handing in my chit, the little man in charge would shove a large stack of papers in front of me. These forms included a certificate of safety, which had to be signed by the engineer in charge; a series of half a dozen or more petrol vouchers which I had to sign, much to the detriment of my scribbling ability (woe be to my hand if no carbon paper were supplied!); a form 700 (daily inspection sheet); and perhaps a few other papers, such as a sealed parcel or clock. After signing away my life, I would cram the logbooks under my arm and find out where the aircraft was. If I were lucky, a ground engineer would carry my parachute, and I could stumble along under a lighter load.

At the plane, the kind man would put my parachute in the cockpit, while I puttered around making an external check of the aircraft. I'd gather all my paraphernalia – helmet and goggles, maps, *Blue Bible* (the small book containing a brief summary of technical data for all aircraft), gloves – have my overnight bag stowed away if necessary, and clamber in. Much energy would be expended in hooking up the parachute and the aircraft harnesses. A few minutes would be given to a thorough cockpit check according to an ATA routine list which covered all the important checks on any type of aircraft.

Here is the list, which we memorized:

ATA Checklist

H – Hydraulics. Power knobs, hydraulic pressure, testing reserve system by flaps.

T – Throttle Tension. Freedom of throttles through complete range, throttle lock or tension wheel check.

T – Trim. Elevator, aileron, and rudder trimmers through complete range and proper settings.

M – Mixture. What type of carburetor and correct starting position.

P – Pitch. Check range of propeller lever and proper starting position according to type of prop- also position and type of feathering control.

P – Petrol. Check contents, gauges, and cocks for all tanks.

F – Flaps. Check movement and indicator.

G – Gills (cowl flaps). Check movement, indicators, and setting for starting.

G – Generators

G – Gauges (instruments)

G – Gyro. Automatic pilot off, test directional gyro.

F – Fuel boosters. Check pressure

U – Unlock controls. Check freedom of controls

S – Superchargers. Check proper setting.

T – Tail wheel lock.

By initials, it can be said, "H, double T, M, double P, F, G₄, F, U, S, T."

"My golly!" exclaims the reader, "You don't do that all the time by memory."

"Well," sez I, "I usually do it twice before every takeoff; if I don't, I'm very likely to have trouble. You can't afford to forget anything."

Some propellers would turn clockwise and some counter-clockwise. You had to remember which way, due to the use of the rudder to counteract the torque involved. With those powerful engines, there is a tendency for the airplane to swing immediately at the beginning of takeoff. You need to correct quickly with the rudder and possibly light braking. If you anticipate the wrong way, it can be a most embarrassing spin off to the side and maybe wiping out the undercarriage!

After this check, I would call "all clear" and "contact!" and hope the engine would start. Sometimes it's rather difficult to do with just two hands. On a Spitfire, for instance, there is a booster coil button and a starter button side by side. Next to it is the "doper," which is a plunger Ki-gas to feed fuel to the cylinders. On the left is the throttle and fuel cut-out lever. Well, we can "dope" the engine and switch on the ignition. Now comes the fun! Usually the engine must be "caught" on the doper, which means that as the engine kicks over, the plunger must be pushed in to get fuel. Also, the booster coil must be held in until the engine is running smoothly, as it provides a spray of sparks to ignite the gases in the cylinder. Then too, the fuel cut-out must remain in its off position until the motor is running and then must be pushed into the rich position so that the fuel will flow steadily. The throttle might have to be moved forward a bit. That means a busy time for a few seconds.

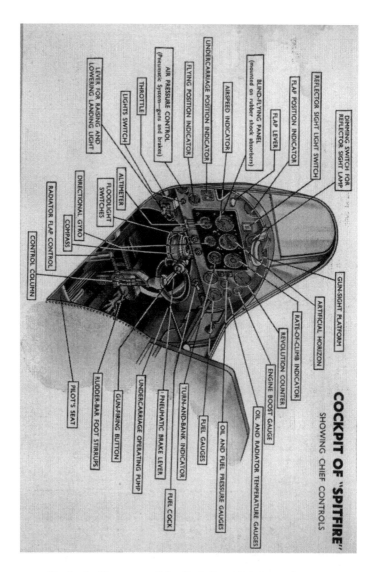

Cockpit diagram of the Spitfire. Origin unknown

In a Barracuda, with help from a Navy crewman

After starting, there would be the oil and fuel pressures to check, plus oil, radiator, or cylinder head temperatures. Then a check to see that the engine-driven hydraulic pumps are working and that there is no dead magneto by checking the ignition switches. After a few more checks and having reached the minimum temperatures, I would "run it up," opening the throttle, checking the pitch and ignition, and doing a power check (certain revolutions at a certain boost or throttle opening). On the Spitfire and some others, this meant two people lying astride the surfaces so that the tail would not rise during the power check.

If everything were okay, I would wave my arms back and forth to have the chocks withdrawn from under the wheels. Then I would taxi out to the takeoff point, checking the tail wheel lock (if any), do a final "H, double T" check, set the compass and directional gyro, clear the engine, get a green light from the control van, taxi onto the runway, lock the tail wheel, and open up.

As you open up, there is a feeling of a surge of power. You are forced back into the seat and must make a definite effort to retain balance. As you get used to this surge, you anticipate it, make the correction beforehand, and hardly notice it on the actual takeoff. The hand is fairly tense on the throttle, the head is set ahead to notice the direction of takeoff and any correction to be made. In a Spitfire, you look side to side, as you can't see ahead at all; in a twin-engine Beaufighter, you are in the nose and have no part of the aircraft for a reference point. The body is tense, anxious that everything will be okay. In the Spit, the rush of air whips into the cockpit, blowing particles up and around. The right hand moves according to the feel of the plane, the tail coming up, the slight pressure back, and becoming airborne. A reach for the landing gear lever, then back to the throttle, a quick glance at the airspeed indicator and engine instruments, then adjustment of everything for the climb.

82

The land falls away at an angle and you are sailing through the air as if by magic. As you look down the wing into space, you feel small, as if an atom or star suspended over an enormous flat quilt of brown, green, gray, and blue, rippling with rolling hills. Overhead, on a good day, you can see the fair-weather cumulus, the big billowing white clouds which seem to be dancing and smiling at you as you fly past.

It is the singular joy of a pilot to let his imagination wander and to enjoy scenes a land-lubber rarely experiences. It is his joy too to sit in a plane all alone, away from all closed spaces, all buildings, all dirt, all humanity and breathe pure clean air free of any vice, any unfriendliness. Flying is an escape from the world. Military flying is different, especially on operations. I'm thinking of ordinary pleasure flying on a good day where the air holds no enemies. Then flying gives you freedom, courage, pride, strength, warmth, and seeing the earth in its natural beauty. You are alone, and **only you** can see and feel as you do. There is very little in the world to compare with it.

Flying from A to B might entail some map reading if it's a new route. If not, I would be enjoying the scenery. If the weather were doubtful, I'd have to be alert to make detours. Arriving at B, I would pull and push numerous tabs and levers according to a landing check and attempt to meet the rushing ground with a minimum of shock. Landing is an art, and when well done, arouses the innermost satisfaction of the soul. Landing can also arouse profane vocabulary beyond all imagination. Ferry pilots seldom make perfect approaches and landings all the time due to flying various aircraft which have different characteristics. Yet they seem to do quite well, for there are few accidents caused by errors in judgment or heavy landings.

Having bounced through my landing, I would taxi up to the proper hut or dispersal area, where a ground engineer (mechanic or helper) would wave me into a parking space. I would cut the engine and snap off all switches. Then I could give a big sigh of relief – the plane was delivered safely in one piece. I'd hop out, only hop is too active a word. I'd clamber out, accompanied by a few groans. In fact, descending from a Barracuda is quite dangerous. Out onto the wing, down one step in the belly (fuselage), then down to the cross-platform of the landing gear, then another long step onto the wheel and a final jump onto the ground. And in the Beaufighter, you collapse the back of the seat, reach up and behind for two bars, and then swing yourself backwards out of the seat. I recall my first Beau when I couldn't find the release and had to read my handling notes in order to find out how to get out of the darn thing!

Either a car would collect me or I would walk with the fitter or engineer to the hut, where I would put my flight time on the form 700. I'd pull out my chit and distribute it correctly, keeping my receipt copy as proof of one more delivery. Then I would take another job or wait for a taxi plane back to base. In the meantime, I'd try to brush up a bit so that I'd look more like a "glamour gal" than a tired bedraggled ferry pilot. Back at Hamble, I'd have a cup of tea, some shortbread, and then walk home.

A cup of tea did I say? Yes, that's right. Edith taught me that bad habit. While in Training Pool, Edie decided that I must learn to drink tea, principally because there was no milk to drink, except in tea and coffee, and the waitresses didn't believe it when you asked for a glass of cold water. So Edie put in lots of milk, lots of sugar, and little tea. As time went on, she decreased the first two measurements and increased the tea strength until I could down a respectable cup of tea. I found it a great help during the cold months when tea was about the only warm drink you could get. And finally, it got so that I not only liked my breakfast cup, but really enjoyed my 4:00 PM cup!

Of course the British say that a good cup of tea depends on the tea itself, the water itself, and how you make it. A strength of one teaspoon to a cup is about right and is dropped into a pre-warmed pot. Then boiling water, not lukewarm, is poured into it. A few minutes later you have a real piping hot beverage. The British use

84

mostly an Indian tea, while the Americans use Chinese. Also the water quality is different in the two countries.

Tea bags? Few have heard of them.

At the controls of a Lockheed Hudson

Contact! Britain!

VIII.

HOSPITALS SHOULD BE THE BEST

In August of 1943, I started a three-day leave in London. After I had stayed in bed for a couple of days with a terrific headache, the American Red Cross gal called in a doctor, who advised moving me to a hospital. I was shifted to a British Red Cross place, but there a doctor suggested that I might possibly have *robera*. That meant nothing to me, but when he interpreted it as German measles, I nearly jumped out of my skin. The slight rash lasted about 48 hours – just until I entered the hospital. But do you think I could get out again? No, sir! I had a full two-week period of medical hell that has never been matched since.

This particular hospital, an isolation one for contagious diseases, was an unbelievable example of so-called modern hospitals. A county-run place, it should have had the very best staff, food, and equipment. Instead, it was badly understaffed by a number of dissatisfied nurses; it had extremely poor food with no special allotments by the Ministry of Food; it had inexperienced operators with incomplete equipment. Never in my life have I seen such chaos.

The doctor wanted an x-ray of my lungs. There were no elevators ("lifts"), so I was wrapped up in blankets, shifted to a stretcher-trolley, taken to the head of the stairs, carried by two little men down two flights of stairs, and put onto another stretcher-trolley. Then I was wheeled outside the building into the fresh, damp air and taken to another building, which looked like an old gymnasium. I was propped up on the end of a cot with my back to the x-ray camera which, incidentally, was a small homemade box not much larger than a newspaperman's camera. No modern x-ray equipment at all.

I was stripped to the waist and held a big cold plate against my chest. The old barn was not heated, and I was chilled within minutes. The two operators- one a doctor's wife who helped out voluntarily and an Austrian woman- held a long discussion on the measurement from the camera to my back. Finally the shot was taken, and I had to do the same thing for a side view, waiting while they inexpertly arranged their "box." I was taken back to my room via the same stairs and same method.

The next day, they told me that one of the shots was blurred and that I must have another taken. This entailed another long, cold trip to the barn. I asked them whether they had any portable equipment. They said "Yes, but only for serious cases." I heard later that a little baby with pneumonia had been taken to the barn for an x-ray and had died after a few days. If this is the sort of government-controlled work that operates in Britain, I thoroughly condemn it.

Also, when I was due to be released, I found that I must wait three days after the doctor's okay, in order that my unit might be informed and someone be sent to *collect* me. It happened that my clothes had been brought to the hospital, and all I needed was to put them on and walk out under my own steam. It took me one complete day of talking to all ranks, from nurses to head matron to doctors to the head doctor, to convince them that I no longer needed to stay and that I was old enough to walk out alone. Why give a person a chance to catch another disease during the next three days?

Food is bad enough in England at times, and also it can be very good and well prepared. At this hospital it was very poorly prepared, there was very little of it, and it wasn't fit food for sick people. The first two days I had to ask for a concoction of my own and tell them how to prepare it simply because they had nothing to serve that fit the soft diet I was supposed to have.

I have told my story to a number of people and asked them whether they have had similar experiences. Some said they had been to hospitals where there was a decent atmosphere. I'm glad of that. I should hate to think that my experience is typical of British hospitals. But most people have told me that British hospitals do not have proper food. I know that my experience has given me no respect for those institutions.

They say, as an excuse, "Remember, it's war-time." That excuse has worn itself out. Some honest people in Britain, when I remark about something and then qualify it by saying, "Of course it's war-time and undoubtedly you had it better pre-war," just smile and say "Don't let that fool you. It's just an excuse. It was just as bad beforehand in most cases." So I wonder!

Later, in December of 1943, I learned about another hospital. I flew too long with a cold and my ear clogged up badly. It was an agonizing pain. The RAF doctor took one look and shook his head. He sent me to ATA headquarters by train, where I was immediately sent to a nearby Canadian hospital. This militarized hospital was a modern, up-to-date, clean, cheerful institution, with all possible medicines, equipment, and specialists. I slept for a week under the influence of sulfa drugs. The room was warm and comfortable. The food was excellent, with meat, vegetables, soups, milk (which I never received in the London hospital), fruit juices, tinned fruits, and candy. The entire atmosphere was pleasant, the other patients were cheerful.

Perhaps some people will say, "Yes, but the Canadian hospital was militarized while the British one was civilian, and naturally the military hospitals received the best of everything." No hospital, civilian or otherwise, should be as bad as I found that London one. It reminds me of 20 to 30 years ago. And they say they haven't enough nurses! Of course not, with the poor conditions and extremely small pay they receive.

In January 1944, after recuperating from my ear trouble, I went back for a flight check. I was class 4 and should have had a checkout on the Wellington, but there were no longer any "Wimpies" in the school. So, although it was not according to Hoyle, I was given the conversion course onto the Lockheed Hudson, class 4 plus. That was fine with me. I enjoyed myself in the plane deemed by the United States to be one of the trickiest, meanest ships in service. It was very easy to find yourself in a ground-loop on takeoff or landing. The ATA instructors insisted on making three-point landings in this plane, which was not built for them. However, there were very few Hudson accidents of this sort. Just as soon as I finished school, though, I reverted back into a much safer wheel landing, which allowed better control during the entire run.

Winter passed with little snow; plenty of rain, fog, and cold; and a bit of flying. Up to January of 1944, I had flown 29 various types of aircraft. Spitfires, twin-engine Oxfords, and Hurricanes were the most numerous on my delivery sheets. I had flown the secret Barracuda, the Royal Navy torpedo plane, which was a funny-looking plane that always surprised us by flying at all. I had a Seamew, a US naval observation plane that the Americans called the Seagull, which had a big Fortress tail and cute little wingtips that turned up sharply at the ends. Also, I had flown the Walrus, an amphibian plane used very successfully by the Air-Sea Rescue. The takeoff was akin to a galloping horse, and flying was the wallowing rolling motion of a boat on rough waters. One of the oldest ships in existence, the Swordfish (an open bi-plane), reminded me of a big lumbering truck. It had been used in the Navy as a torpedo plane, being the main power for many years.

I had flown many marks of Spitfires, my favorite of which was the mark XI, a photo reconnaissance plane. It carried no armament and for that reason had very clean lines. Its 1500 horsepower engine gave it great speed, and somehow the controls were perfect. Also, I was partial to the pretty blue camouflage it had! I had flown a little Auster, known as a Taylorcraft in the USA, souped up to 130 horsepower. It had a great deal of Plexiglas, as it was used by specially trained artillery men for spotting. It had three flap settings besides neutral and, with the correct setting, a pilot could take off and land in an amazingly small space.

I had handled the controls of a B-17 Fortress while my commanding officer and pilot, Miss Gore, enjoyed the scenery. I always grin at the recollection of the startled, unbelieving expressions of the RAF ground crew as Miss Gore, her flight engineer Miss Parker, and four women passengers stepped out. They kept looking for a man to come out and, as none appeared, resigned themselves to realizing the flight had been made by an all-woman crew.

Incidents/accidents or close calls? Fortunately I had nothing really serious happen to me, although I think we all had a few rather close calls, with engines or aircraft not performing correctly or poor weather. Weather was always a problem and necessitated quite a few unscheduled landings. Fortunately there were numerous airstrips available, many of which were grass surfaces. We had no radios, so we could not call anyone.

In poor weather, we might fly around for a bit, trying to get through the weather, and then land at the first aerodrome we saw. That is what happened when I landed at Peterborough, an active American B-17 base- I was just glad to get down safely. I was unable to get off for two days due to poor visibility, but the B-17s went out in the morning—and unfortunately not all came back. It was not a happy occasion.

And of course, as mentioned earlier, there was my Spitfire experience with the low clouds. How did I get into that position? I didn't start to think until the bank was already severe. I certainly wasn't pleased with myself. But blinking my eyes and gaining control of my thoughts, I managed to concentrate on the instruments. I had to. It was one of the hardest things I ever had to do, not to look outside. I brought the left wing up to a 30-degree bank and stopped the descent about 400 feet above the ground, climbed back to 600 feet, and then tried to remember my compass reading when entering the cloud. I had not looked at it but guessed at the reading from my previous flight path. I completed what I thought was a 180-degree turn and straightened the aircraft out to straight and level.

It seemed like forever flying back through the clouds. I didn't have time to think of a negative outcome. But almost as suddenly as I had entered it, I flew out of the solid cloud into the still-miserable gray sky. It only took a few minutes more to locate an airport and land. Thank heavens for those few hours of instrument training! The 180-degree turn was a basic maneuver, basic instrument flying, and a basic fight for survival. Amen!

I did have to fill out a form 765 one day. That was an accident form. It isn't so bad that you have an accident; the worst is all the red tape and written work that must be done afterwards. In fact as I sat up there in the Spitfire, I didn't think so much of how I would land- I just cursed the fact that I couldn't fly any more that day (I had to have a medical check) and that I'd have so much writing to do.

I took off in my Spitfire with the green downlights showing. I selected wheels up, but no red lights came on to indicate that the wheels were locked up. So I stooged around the sky for about fifteen minutes trying the lever up and down to get the proper lights. No luck. Well, that continued for a while, then I gave it the "bottle." A bottle of CO_2, released with the selector in down position, should force the wheels all the way down and the locks should engage. But still no lights. Flying slowly across the airfield, I got a "thumbs up" sign from the engineer, indicating that the wheels were down, but of course there was no guarantee that they were locked. I was naturally hoping that only the lights were "U/S."

So I tightened my harness and made the landing. I felt the two wheels touch evenly and breathed a sigh of relief. Then I started working frantically – the starboard wheel had collapsed. I pumped the left brake lever gently, holding the stick hard back, and the plane went very slightly off to the right, digging the wingtip. As it slowed down, it turned almost gently around to 60 degrees from my touchdown, and I switched off the ignition. The port wheel remained up, tire okay, and the prop wasn't even touched. The starboard wingtip, flap, and tailplane were slightly damaged. I hopped out in a hurry, cursing my luck that I had to give up a second job that day. They found out that the downlock had been blocked by foreign matter and wouldn't engage. I was amazed at the smoothness of the one-wheel landing. There was no jarring at all with the tight harness. But I did so hate to see the lovely beauty drooping to one side with a broken leg.

Bundled up to fly the Fairey "Swordfish"

In the cockpit of the "Big Fish" Barracuda

With another Spitfire

As the months progressed, I noticed that I was working harder. In April, I flew 18 different types of aircraft, including six twin-engine planes, three RAF fighters, two Navy fighters, four Navy torpedo planes, two air-sea rescue amphibians, and a small taxi plane. I had several new types, including a Grumman Avenger (TBF); a Sea Otter, similar to a Walrus; a Typhoon, one of the fastest of the British fighters; a Beaufighter, a heavily armed twin-engine torpedo- and rocket-firing Coastal Command plane that has caused great havoc amongst enemy shipping; a Vega Ventura (B-34), big sister to the Hudson; a Corsair, a fast Navy fighter used with great success by American Marine fliers; a Mosquito, thought to be one of the fastest fighter-bombers in the world, a twin-engine plane carrying 4,000 pounds in its sleek belly and as lovely on the controls as a Spitfire; and a Stinson Reliant, the old American civilian job used by the Royal Navy for navigational training.

The Planes We Flew

Special authorizations were given by our commanding officer to fly some advanced or unusual aircraft, such as the Typhoon fighter, the newer and more powerful models of the Spitfire, or the amphibious Walrus. We did not land in the water, only on land, hopefully wheels down. However, there were a few men additionally qualified for seaplanes. My last checkout was in an Albemarle, a twin-engine with a tri-cycle gear. At this time, that gear was an oddity. Only a few, such as the B-25 Mitchell, were outfitted with the nose wheel in front; most had tailwheels.

The authorization included a review by the instructor to check on our progress to date and to be sure that we hadn't acquired too many bad habits. It was a remarkably efficient check-out program. I ended up with about nine dual checkouts over a period of about a year, and I flew 41 types solo or as PIC (pilot in command) first time up.

No American woman I know of ferried the Meteor jet, which was out just at the end of the war, or converted to the four-engines, although eleven of the British women were qualified to fly the Halifax, Lancaster, Stirling, B-17, and B-24. Veronica Volkersz (British) was the first woman to ferry the Meteor. No women, either in the ATA or WASP, flew as pilot in command across the Atlantic during World War II.

I did fly across the Atlantic, as did some others, while returning from leave in the US in 1944. While I was classified as third pilot, I never saw the cockpit. I had to ride near the bomb-bay, where there was an oxygen outlet. Although warmly dressed in a sitcot (fleece flying suit), I was still cold—and had problems trying to undress enough to relieve myself into a small can, with an oxygen mask on at 25,000 feet and cold drafts coming through the unheated part of the aircraft!

Several times in April and May of 1945, we were given specific orders to fly into our restricted area only over a certain route. This, plus the great amount of shipping which we saw, gave us false hopes that the invasion was taking place. The tenseness that built up during those two months was astonishing. We found ourselves looking at one another but not speaking about the ships in the harbor, exchanging gossip more seriously, guessing where and when the blow would take place, as were millions of others.

On June 4th, I noticed at an American station that all the P-47 Thunderbolts were being given an overcoat of three broad white and two black stripes across each wing and around the fuselage. One soldier, who shouldn't have said it, remarked that they had worked all night on them and probably would have to do it again that evening in order to complete the job. On the 5th of June, flying over a familiar aerodrome, I noticed that it was jammed with gliders and their power machines, mostly Douglas C-47 (DC-3) airplanes, all with the big "invasion stripes" painted on them. I have never seen such a crowded place. Gliders were all over the field on the grass, in dispersal areas, hangars, and in far parking spaces. Only by being directly over the runways could you distinguish them out of the maze of aircraft. These two clues gave me a hint that something was going to pop soon. But I didn't expect it the next day.

I woke up at 5:00 AM on June 6th. My ears buzzed. Sleepily, I turned on the lights, saw the time, groaned, and shook my head vigorously. Then, as consciousness came to my aid, I realized that there was a terrific flight of B-17 Fortresses going overhead. It was a steady thundering roar. I remember wondering whether it would be that way on "D" Day. When I dozed off around 5:30, the roar was still there. At 8:30, when I caught the bus to the aerodrome from my new billet, I saw dirty low clouds and still heard the mass of Forts going across. A few sections chose to fly low under the cloud, and they made a stirring sight.

At 9:00 AM, just as I walked onto the field, the field broadcast system blared out with the 9:00 o'clock news, stating that the Germans claimed the invasion had begun. You can be sure that there was tension and excitement in the ATA hut as various reports came in that morning. However, after General Eisenhower's confirmation, the tension seemed to vanish and a sort of anxiety appeared in its place. It was such a disappointment when the chits came out to find the same usual routine jobs. I believe everyone there had romantic but vain thoughts that there would be spectacular life-saving jobs to squadrons. We had done our work several months previously, although we didn't know it at the time.

Just before we set out to work that day, we rushed out onto the airfield in time to see an operational Spitfire making a circuit in the wrong direction. It sort of wobbled onto the field and bounced along precariously. Finally it slithered to a halt, paused a few minutes, and then slowly turned around and taxied back. The ambulance and crash wagon had given full chase down the rough grass surface. Evidently, the pilot wasn't badly hurt, for he continued to the parking dispersal area at the other end of the field. For the next few days, one or two shot-up Spits would force-land, fortunately without much damage. It gave us a sensation of being pretty near the front, which we were – only 28 miles of water separated us from France.

Third Officer Nancy Miller, 1942

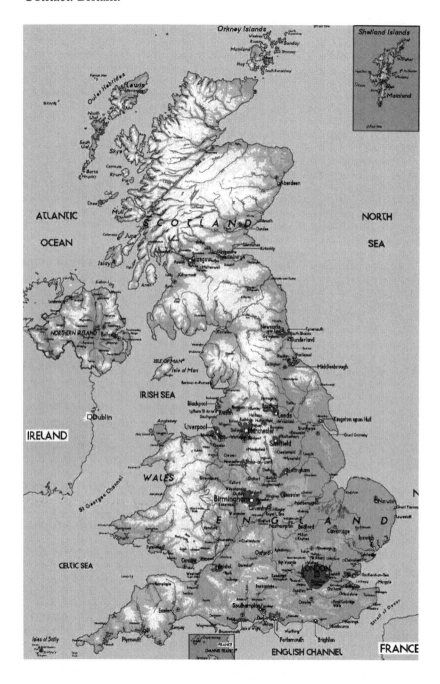

IX.

YA CANNA CALL THIS ENGLAND

I had always wanted to go to Scotland, but for some unknown reason I never flew that far north. I had made inquiries as to whether I could be seconded to Prestwick, just south of Glasgow, for a couple of months, but no definite answer was forthcoming. In the middle of June 1944, however, a notice appeared to the effect that a women's flight was to be organized at Prestwick and all those interested should give their names to adjutant. This I did. So did Vera, the Danish girl. We wanted to go there because of the reputation it had for twin-engine aircraft. Since Hamble was essentially what we call a single-engine pool, we wanted more experience on the two-motor ships. How ironical it was to go up there and find that Prestwick had reverted more to single-engines again and that twins were scarce!

Before I left Hamble, I had two new types. One was a marvelous, popular American bomber, the Douglas A-20 or "Boston." This was my first real experience with a tricycle landing gear. In a rather strong cross-wind it handled beautifully, with easy directional control. The other plane, also American, was the Grumman F6F Hellcat, a Navy fighter and successor to the F4F Wildcat. Despite a close circuit due to bad weather, it behaved nicely.

The first week in July, I drove with Jean Bird some 400 miles by car up to Prestwick. Her little eight-horsepower Morris, loaded down by baggage in the rumble seat ("dicky"), chugged up hills, purred down hills, and wobbled on all turns. We switched places every two hours, and it was quite an experience to check out British roads in a British car. We had one blowout, when we changed tires and were on our way again in ten minutes. It was a tiring trip, due to the continuous curving of the roads. There are few straight parts of more than a quarter of a mile and very few three-lane highways in Britain. Most of their roads follow the old Roman trails, which were built around fields and according to the land's natural contours, providing narrow, winding roadways.

As we drove up to the ATA building at Prestwick, Ann Blackwell climbed out of her car and Vera, who had flown up, jumped out of a van. Thus the four of us, starting at different times, all arrived at 4 PM.

The following day provided a rather unusual entrance for three of us newcomers. Ann was to pick up Vera and me at 8:45 AM. At 9:00 there was no sign of Ann, and the two of us were very worried, as 9:15 was the deadline and it took about twelve minutes to drive out. As we fumed the minutes away, as well as two possible lifts, suddenly a huge Rolls Royce stopped beside us. Imagine our surprise when Ann popped her head out of the side window.

"Hurry!" she said, waving us in. "My car broke down, so my billetor arranged for this private car to take us to the aerodrome." Stunned, we climbed aboard. Away we sped and pulled up in front of the ATA hut just at 9:16. Imagine our embarrassment upon making our debut at Prestwick in a Rolls Royce! An auspicious beginning!

I had heard that the Scottish people are friendlier than the English. I have found several nice families in each country, and yet I have seen rudeness in each too. Vera's and Jean's billetors were very nice, as were most of the Scottish men working for ATA. I found the latter very kind, friendly, and helpful, even though some of them had such broad accents that I couldn't understand them! But I think the Scottish accent is most delightful and prefer it to the English. Of course, they all get a kick out of our various American accents!

In July and August Scotland was quite warm, although rain often poured down in torrents – not a light drizzle, but like a good eastern US summer thunderstorm. People from Glasgow on vacation swarmed all over the narrow beaches at Ayr and Prestwick. I never got up enough nerve to take a dip into the sea, but Vera did. She swam around for about five minutes and then turned to come in. Suddenly we spotted an animal swimming toward a rock near her. She was somewhat startled but reached the beach. We watched the baby seal climb on top of the rock. I'm sure he was making fun of Vera's swimming, for after Vera came in and stood watching, it seemed as if he laughed at her and then plopped lazily into the sea and swam off.

The geography of Scotland was entirely different from England. The highlands in the north rose majestically and forbiddingly to a pilot, and a hill only a few miles from Prestwick rose to 1,230 feet. However in the Midlands there were only a few rolling hills of 500 to 600 feet, with one peak of 900 feet.

The more hilly Scottish terrain necessitated a flying route up the Perth Valley north of Glasgow over to the east coast and then a northwesterly course to arrive at one of the popular delivery points. Very seldom, unauthorized trips were made over the top of the highlands. If a forced landing were to be made, there would be practically no hope of getting out alive. The mountains, although midgets compared to the US ranges, were gorgeous in their green coats. There were a few bare spots of brown, and sometimes you could find little deep blue lakes ("lochs") right on top of a ridge. In the winter time, most of these highlands were covered with snow. Loch Lomond, perhaps the most famous of the Scottish lochs, is an unequalled sight on a beautiful summer's day. Ben Lomond rises to one side of the loch, blending into highlands. The loch itself is a deep, rich blue, with little green island top-knots irregularly spaced in the loch.

The men at the pool were quite friendly, but as no other women had been posted there, some skepticism was noticeable. Our jobs were not the best at first, and sometimes our patience was tried sorely, but we just plugged along. Eventually more girls were posted to Prestwick, and the men came to accept them. The commanding officer and second-in-command admitted they were rather amazed that the women could fly all the machines as well as they did, although some women had been doing it for a long, long time. It took about two months to be treated as pilots, but once accepted, they gave us an equal share of all jobs.

The jobs at Prestwick were longer, and thus we flew a few more hours with fewer deliveries. The jobs weren't particularly interesting and often entailed long rides back in an Anson. This called for a heavy coat, gloves, scarf, and boots in order to keep any warmth in the body. I had a few new types. I flew a Warwick, big brother to the Wellington. It had either two 2,000-horsepower Double Wasp engines or two 2,400-horsepower Centaurus engines and weighed around 42,500 pounds (ferrying load). Despite the weight, it took off after a short run and climbed well.

As I flew it, I thought of the old classification we used to have in the States: class 1, class 2 (1,500-4,000 pounds), class 3S (single engine) and 3M (multi-engine, from 4,000-10,000 pounds), class 4M (10-25,000 pounds) and class 5 (over 25,000 pounds). It never occurred to me when flying my little class-one planes that I should ever have the chance or be qualified to fly in the highest classification. Zero to 80 horsepower is my present frozen rating at home, but even thinking about the newer horsepower ratings that we have in the US, according to the planes I've flown in the ATA, I'd have a single and multi-engine land rating from 0 to 7200 horsepower.

I was at Prestwick, being helped into a Navy Barracuda torpedo plane with my parachute by one of the flight engineers, when I realized that I was not in England, as we Americans generally call the islands here. He asked me where I was off to, and I said, "near Chester." Oh," he replied in his thick Scottish brogue, "You're flying to England!" as if it were 1,000 miles away, another country. I hadn't thought much about it, with Chester being only about an hour south, but the route did cross the Scottish/English border. That is a very definite distinction. So, while in Scotland "you canna call this England."

I should mention that along the way, with our progression in experience, we also advanced in rank. We started training as cadets, with one narrow stripe on our shoulder lapel. Then we advanced to third officer, one broad stripe, and second officer, a narrow and a broad stripe. Sometime during my stay at Hamble, I became a first officer, roughly equivalent to an Army captain rank, with two broad stripes. Advancement beyond this, to flight captain, was reserved for administrative or section leaders.

Row, Row, Row Your Boat

Our dark blue uniform with gold wings and gold stripes confused many people. The ATA is not well known, so we are continually besieged with questions. Jackie Sorour, from South Africa, had the best experience along that line. Jackie was stopped by a woman and asked the usual question. Jackie replied, "I'm a ferry pilot." The woman thought a minute and then burst out with understanding,

"Oh, you ferry the boats down the Thames. How nice!" and turned away in all ignorance.

As to salaries, for the first officers it was about $1,900 to $2,300 per year. Ms. Cochran also very wisely included in our 18-month contract $25 per week to be sent to a US bank of our choice. Commander Pauline Gower went to Parliament and obtained equal pay for the women. The women also had seniority pay according to their service, the same as the men. All pilots had the same insurance and medical care. Flying jobs were given (mostly!) without regard for sex, flying experience being the main criterion. There didn't seem to be the same antagonism toward women pilots in the ATA that there was in the US.

It was on August 16th that I had one of my greatest thrills. Sentiment has placed a great value on the DC-3, or C-47, the Douglas mainliner of US airlines. Here was another plane that had awed me in my more inexperienced days. Now I was to fly it with a flight engineer by my side. From the cockpit I looked down the wings, and they looked awfully long. I sort of gulped and got on with the job. First, my engineer shot my picture from the ground with me hanging out of the cockpit window. (It was still against rules to have cameras on aerodromes!) Then we started up the engines and taxied out. I slipped on headphones and heard the Prestwick tower talking away in the British manner. Off we went.

The ATA trained 151 flight engineers, of whom four were women, to help with the more complex twin-engine planes, as well as all of the four-engine aircraft. There were not enough pilots to have co-pilots, so either a flight engineer went along on certain aircraft or else an RAF cadet (the 17 to 18-year-old lads) would go along to help with the landing gear or emergency controls that might be out of reach of the pilot. Although the engineer is not a pilot, he usually likes to take the controls in the air. He learns quite a bit by this method, and I believe that some of the older hands could bring down a plane safely in an emergency.

I contend the engineer does all the work. I simply flicked my hand thus, and up came the landing gear. After gaining single-engine speed, I flicked my fingers, and the engineer brought back the throttles and pitch levers to climbing position. Gaining a thousand feet, about all I could do because of lowish clouds, I flicked my fingers again and everything came back to the cruising position. I trimmed up the aircraft to fly hands-off, double-checked all instruments, and relaxed. The engineer, bless his heart, turned on the command set to a station that was really giving out with the old 12th Street Rag, one of my favorites. We both listened to an extremely good swing program, and he took over the controls while I relaxed even more.

As we continued down the coast, I noticed the cloud forming on our right. There were small patches beneath us too. It looked fairly clear ahead and to the left, which was our route, so I didn't worry much. Suddenly, though, the ground disappeared, my last glance being of WF aerodrome almost directly beneath us. I took over, changed course, and attempted to drop beneath the cloud. I found it quite solid, so I immediately climbed above it into the clear. That is, it should have been clear, but it wasn't, so I found myself flying on instruments—which, as mentioned before, is not only against ATA rules but rather risky without thorough training. I had had about 15 hours now on a Link trainer and four hours under the hood in an airplane. That included some practice on the Prestwick range and let-down procedure.

I flew by the compass, making sure I was heading out to sea, not into the mountains. I kept climbing, and at about 1800 feet I came out on top again. Both of us looked for a hole, but the lovely white and gray mass below us didn't look at all promising. I had the command set turned back onto the Prestwick frequency, figuring that I could at least fly back there if need be. Then suddenly I spotted a hole and immediately dove through it, coming out at 300 feet over the sea. The hole was over a small inlet that I knew, so I turned back onto my reciprocal to hit the coast and then to the west to land at WF. I wriggled the C-47 back and forth in order to see the mile ahead, all the visibility that we had.

Finally, at 400 feet altitude, I spotted the airfield, made a short circuit, narrowly missing an Anson that was also just landing. Patches of cloud flew past as the engineer lowered the landing gear. I was still flying mainly by instruments, only looking out to catch the sight of the red marker beacon, which indicated the beginning of the runway in use. As I came in, I was still flying through cloud bits at 200 feet and peering through the smoke-haze to line up correctly. I was slightly off to the right, but a firm turn brought the Dakota nicely in line and she sat down smoothly.

Naturally, both of us were quite relieved to be on the ground. Later that day, when the cloud lifted and the visibility became better, we took off and completed the delivery. I learned later that Prestwick had closed in just about the time I landed at WF and that we probably would not have been able to get in there. Ah well, such is flying (especially in British weather!) and such is luck. And quite exciting for the first time in a new type!

July and August were fairly warm months, and flying was fair. Vera had a forced landing in a Navy "Firefly," which enlivened things a bit. The engine cut after she had made a circuit, and due to her position she had to land about half-way down the runway. She couldn't get the flaps down, although the wheels lowered okay, so her hot landing took her right off the end of the runway. In order to avoid a brick wall and some people nearby, she ground-looped deliberately, wiped off the undercarriage, but did very little other damage. She didn't have a scratch. We had to laugh too. Ten days previously, she had sprained her ankle badly while ice skating. However, in this airplane accident, she didn't even have a bruise. We warned her to stay away from the ice rink! It was dangerous.

Actually my closest call in ATA came not during my Spitfire accident but in a near accident. On August 31, 1944, I had a Wellington bomber to return from the south up to Scotland. This day my "Wimpy" was particularly ornery. There was a fairly strong cross-wind from the right, which I noticed, so that as the tail rose and the nose suddenly shot to the right, I almost expected it. But I didn't expect it to be so vicious. I opened up the starboard throttle, but my ears told me that the engine was not producing the correct power. I slammed back the port throttle, and the instant the machine straightened I closed both of them. I was off the runway but parallel to it. I applied the brakes, as I didn't have much more room. Groaning and praying, I ran off the end of the runway and finished ten feet from a small workman's hut. Looking at my brake gauge I shuddered as I saw it at 60 pounds, way below minimum safe limits.

So thinking it was just my fault with the cross wind, I revved up the port engine to build the brake pressure and taxied down for another try. I revved up the engines to #4 (38" Hg.) boost but not to full power at #8¼ (46½" Hg.). Everything seemed okay, so trying once more I started extremely slowly and was particularly careful about the throttles. Just as the tail came up, wham! around she went to starboard again. I gave full starboard throttle and glanced at the instruments. In an instant, I saw the boost differing as it should, port #4, starboard #8¼, but—and my mind took a whirl—the rpm of both engines was only about 2,350-2,400 (takeoff rpm = 2,850). Naturally, the cross-wind would affect the huge plane, as really there was no variance of engine power to counteract it.

Despite this very brief glance, when I looked up again, I was too far down the runway to stop this time. I pulled back the port engine a bit more, slammed on as much left rudder as I could and, having gained takeoff speed, yanked her off just as the machine was turning about thirty degrees off the runway. I knew I couldn't quite control her, although I was trying hard enough. I didn't dare give any more left engine, as it would only aggravate the turning, and I didn't want to feather the right one because I didn't have enough speed, and I still had some power from it. As the swing got worse, veering off to about 60 degrees at about 200 feet altitude and skidding a little sideways, I gained single-engine speed and was just reaching over to feather the starboard engine when, wham! the whole machine shook and slithered violently around to the opposite side. I grabbed the throttles, equalized them as I pulled them back, adjusted the pitch levers for climbing, opened the gills wider, and read the instruments for any further signs of irregularity. Strangely enough, everything behaved itself, although I circled the field for about fifteen minutes before starting cross-country. A smooth landing at my destination restored my confidence a bit.

I still remember those houses I would have piled into if I hadn't gained control. Those houses are very vivid indeed. Luckily, that engine picked up, or I probably never would have been able to say that the engine sputtered. And it taught me to check each engine more fully (when possible), not just part throttle, and not to take off with brake pressure low. Fortunately, I learned and lived; it could have been a lesson in vain if that Hercules engine hadn't percolated again.

Fired On

Many pilots have seen the puffs of ack-ack or perhaps a distant enemy plane. But some have gotten much closer to danger. An Anson load of pilots was attacked by two ME-109s near White Waltham and, according to Betty Hayman, who was one of the passengers, they came close enough for the passengers to see the whites of their eyes. Jim Mollison, the pilot, pulled the Anson up into the ever-present clouds and escaped that way. Kay Van D. flew nonchalantly across Bournemouth one day just at the time it was being bombed. Vera Strodl landed at a secret airfield without seeing a couple of enemy aircraft several thousand feet overhead.

Edith Stearns had a few exciting adventures with enemy aircraft and the V-1 buzz bombs. On her first ferry delivery in a Hurricane in 1942, in the usual bad weather, she spied a plane coming up behind her at a slight angle. She watched it in the rear-view mirror, thinking only of avoiding it if it flew in too closely. Suddenly she saw the black Swastika. There was little for her to do. Unarmed and untrained in combat maneuvers, she would be no match for the Germans. This was one time she was thankful for the "usual bad weather" and her previous instrument training. She pulled up into the clouds and flew on instruments for a few minutes. When she let down, the Hun had disappeared. Upon landing at her destination, the ground crew told her that an air raid was on. Seems that she had flown right through lots of ack-ack, as well as almost being attacked by the enemy plane!

During 1944, when so many of the V-1 buzz bombs appeared over southern England, Edie had another close experience. Following a special route in poor visibility, she was suddenly startled by the concussion of ack-ack. Puffs of smoke appeared all around her. In poor weather it is difficult for the ground batteries to distinguish planes and V-1s. Under such conditions, she was supposed to lower her wheels so that the batteries could spot her. However, it takes a while for a Spitfire to slow down from its fast cruising speed to the maximum speed to lower the undercart. She decided just to plow onwards and trust to luck. When she arrived at her destination, Grace Stevenson and some others rushed out to her and exclaimed excitedly,

"Edie, you just missed it! A V-1 just went over the airfield."

Edie retorted, not too calmly,

"Oh, no I didn't. I was shot at!" It appeared that the paths of the Spit and the V-1 had crossed and thus she had been in direct line of the ground firing.

The only time anyone shot at me was friendly fire when I was flying a Spitfire up near Greenock, Scotland, base for the big battleships and for the Queen Mary and Queen Elizabeth, which were being used as troop transports. I came too close to the harbor, and suddenly heavy ack-ack appeared to my left. I kinda gulped and turned away. But unlike what some other pilots experienced, they were **not** shooting **at** me, just—ah—limiting my curiosity. Kind of shooing me away. It was still a little frightening

X.

THE STREETS OF OLD NEW YORK

On September 2, 1944, the assistant adjutant called me in and said, "Do you want to go home?"

"What do you mean by 'home'?" I asked suspiciously.

"The United States," she replied, rather impatiently.

"Well," I drawled, "I think it would be very nice. Why?"

"The ban is off now, and headquarters asked if you still wanted to go back this year for your leave." There had been an exit ban in England, which had prevented any American from the usual home leave the ATA allowed us. I had been wanting this trip since March.

"You bet I want to go," I said emphatically, "What's to do?"

There followed five days of hectic arranging, packing, renewal of passport, and getting an exit permit, plus flying. Naturally, I was most excited and happy. On September 11th, I went through the very tiring, boring, and inefficient Customs and was swept out to the

113

Queen Elizabeth. She was a stirring sight, the largest ship afloat. Luckily, I hadn't brought many suitcases, just two with a small overnight bag. We stepped across the boards from the launch, a sort of ferry boat, and into an enormous clean white passageway.

I was rather awed and stood shock-still, until a pleasant steward came up and took my baggage and put me on the elevator. From it, I stepped into a sort of squarish center, with passageways leading in four directions down the length of the ship and broad stairs leading up onto the promenade deck. There another man, this time an RAF officer, took me in charge, secured my berth ticket (in front of a long queue of men) and showed me to my stateroom. It was on the main deck, fairly well forward.

There were three other women in the room. This was quite good, as there were four sets of triple bunks in the room and only a side-squeezing space down the middle. The two portholes could be left open during the daytime but had to be closed at night, as there was a complete blackout. There was a salt-water bath, which I tried once with no success. Hot fresh water was brought in each morning and night by our steward.

On the docks, I had met six ATA Canadian boys and a dozen or so transatlantic ferry pilots. I was the only woman pilot aboard and one of the few dozen women altogether. I met many Americans, most of whom were wounded boys being sent back home. I met one or two nurses whom I had met in the London Nurses' Club. There were some US Navy boys going home on leave too and a few RAF officers who helped in the running of the troops. There were also quite a number of German prisoners, none of whom believed they were on the Queen Elizabeth, as it had been sunk three or four times by the Germans!

As we had boarded the ship around 3:00 PM, we were slightly hungry. However a meal was ready for us, and we walked down half a mile of corridor and down three flights of stairs in order to find the mess hall. At least we were sure of having an appetite. The elevators could be used by lieutenant colonels, lieutenant commanders, or wing commanders (and higher ranks), the wounded, and women. I only used it once or twice, figuring the exercise was good for me.

The meals on the Queen Elizabeth were little short of heaven. After two years of British food, the fresh vegetables (such as sweet corn and peas), the white flour rolls, the large pieces of meat, and the fruit were magnificent. We had only two meals a day, but they were sufficient with the rolls which we slipped out for snacks. By the time I had finished six days on the ship, I had somewhat satisfied myself as to food.

The trip itself was smooth, and after a day out, the sun shone and it became quite hot, much to my pleasure. We could tell we were leaving Britain. The warmth made sleeping a bit difficult, especially with the closed portholes. Walking on the decks was pleasant though a bit crowded. The lounge was a huge room filled with all sorts of people, with two special tables of red-hot American poker players. It rather surprised me to see what I had often heard of, three and four hundred dollars bet on a single hand. One boy told me he didn't figure he could enter a game unless he had a thousand dollars in his pocket! So the British play darts and call Americans "crackers" (nuts), and I sometimes don't blame them!

There were many wounded boys aboard. Many were on stretchers on various decks, while some hobbled around on the boat deck. One colonel had been blinded but he, with a friend, walked briskly up and down in the sunshine and wind. Several were on crutches but managed to get around beautifully. One boy at my dinner table had lost several fingers and was re-learning to use a knife and fork. His foot was bandaged too, where shrapnel had injured it. In fact, he had 52 wounds! He mentioned how happy and interested he had been when the famous reporter Ernie Pyle had come into his ward and talked to him and the rest of the boys. Ernie looked very tired, but he still kept on a smile and visited the boys as often as he could.

I visited one ward of 150 stretcher cases. They had casts on, some had limbs tied up by cables, many had no legs or arms, some were almost completely bandaged. But they were happy – they were going home. A little red-haired boy with one leg provided many laughs and was the life of the party. Yet just opposite him was a boy in a chest cast who had a wry smile and not much hope. He was still suffering from shock. He didn't joke. He said, "I'm so afraid they'll send me back again and I don't want go." I asked the nurse about him, but she said that he wouldn't be well for at least a year. However, he didn't seem to believe that. There were many of those boys who didn't want to go back, but very few admitted it.

The nurse told me afterwards that the slight smell which I had encountered upon entering the ward was almost unbearable by the end of the trip, six days later. Casts could not be changed, and one boy had a bad leg which infected a cast and stank worse each day. Nothing could be done. As usual, everyone joked about it, and the embarrassed boy grinned away everything except the stink.

We missed a hurricane that swept up the eastern coast and continued our smooth trip into New York harbor on Sunday, the 17th. I got a front seat on the port side so that I could be thrilled when viewing the Statue of Liberty. When I saw her, I was disappointed. She had on a dull, unbecoming green dress. Nothing, not even a spark, arose in me, so I made my way through the mass of humanity to the other side. There my heart warmed and beat faster as I saw the skyline of New York. It was a magnificent sight, New York standing tall and proud and majestic. It meant more to me than the "Old Lady" herself.

Fortunately, government officials and ferry pilots were allowed off the boat first. Some of the boys had to remain until 9 at night. There were few people to greet us. A band played some pieces, and a women's voluntary service served coffee or milk and luscious sugared doughnuts, the American kind. Our kits (bags) were taken off while we passed through the Customs and FBI officials in the lounge.

Then we scampered off, inhaling deeply of American air, and had our baggage checked.

We had a car to take us to the Wentworth Hotel. Some of the boys went off that night on trains, but as I wished to collect my traveling expenses and also make arrangements to fly to Los Angeles, I stayed overnight. The first thing I wanted to do was to buy some ice cream, but somehow I didn't. I went out to LaGuardia to see about getting a priority to fly. The lieutenant heard my story and granted my request, but when I found I didn't have enough money to fly that night, I had to wait until Monday.

I went back to New York proper in the luxury of a real cab. The power those cars had! I could hardly realize it after being in so many eight-to-10-horsepower British vehicles. That night, after a good hotel dinner with plenty of pleasant, helpful waitress service and a double helping of ice cream, I wandered onto the streets of New York.

The most startling impression I received was as I came to Fifth Avenue and looked down towards Times Square. Lights, thousands of them- daylight at 9:00 PM. Flashing newsreels, ten movie houses, lights in cafes, lights in show windows, bright lights on cars. It would be a magic and unbelievable sight to any five-year-old child of Britain who had never known anything but blackouts. It was magic to me, who had not seen them in two years.

I just stood and watched the lights and the lively, jostling crowds. Life just seemed to be beginning at 9:00 or 10:00 PM. In Britain, things were beginning to close up, what few things still ran at that time of night, and there are no lights to indicate any life at all. I stood peering in at the café where you just put nickels and dimes in a slot to get certain appetizing dishes. There was no restaurant like that in Britain, no such foods, not many such happy and contented faces.

I started to cross a street. I looked the wrong way and the blare of a loud horn sent me back to the curb. Such loud noises, I thought. I grinned at the recollection of the London taxies with their little rubber-squeeze horns attached to the sides of the windshields. I started off again, noticing traffic a block away. I didn't hurry until more blaring of horns sent me scooting for the other side. I had forgotten that Americans drive much faster than the British.

When I walked back to the hotel, it felt as though my circulation had begun to do double time. I enjoyed my private room with bath and was just turning on the water when I noticed there was a shower attached. There are very few showers in Britain and not much hot water to have one. So I settled in to enjoy the luxury of an extended hot shower, thinking all the time of wasting water. It took me about two weeks to get over that feeling. Everything was available in such quantity that the comparison with Britain made me realize how fortunate USA was.

The next morning, BOAC paid out the airline fare and expense money, whereupon I dashed out to LaGuardia, procured my priority ticket, and hopped the five-o'clock plane for home. Upon landing at Pittsburgh, I rang up my aunt. The shock was almost too much for her, and she bawled me out for not letting her know that I was coming in on the plane. Practically the same thing happened at Chicago, where my cousin was quite astonished to hear my voice. This convinced me that perhaps I should notify my father instead of walking in on him. I sent the telegram that night, and my stepmother told me afterwards that he was shocked beyond words when he received it.

As usual, the meals were served on board and were extremely good. Even the snacks early in the morning proved to be much better than the usual run of food in Britain. No fault of the British; it was just the way things were.

The beautiful and elegant Supermarine Spitfire

DeHavilland Mosquito bomber, the "Mossie"

Fairey Albacore

Hawker Tempest fighter

Bristol Beaufighter

Fairey Battle

Hawker Hurricane

Hawker Typhoon

Fairchild 24 used for transport to/from other flights

Auster, the RAF equivalent to the Taylorcraft

Westland Lysander observation aircraft

The odd-looking De Havilland Dominie transport

American P-51 Mustang (an "F" model)

F4U Corsair

Grumman TBM/Avenger

Grumman Hellcat

Douglas A-20 Boston attack bomber

Vickers Wellington bomber

Contact! Britain!

XI.

HOME IS WHERE THE HEART IS

It was a warm tingling feeling to alight at Burbank, where I had landed in a Luscombe years before. The airline limousine took me to the Hollywood ticket office, where I saw my father walking restlessly. Suddenly little Linda, my niece (only she wasn't so small anymore), dashed around the corner into my arms. Then my brother Dick and Duds, his wife, came into view, little Janice, then Dad and Priscilla. What a reunion! I had to borrow 15 cents from Dick to help pay for the limo fare. Some homecoming!

We drove to Dick's house where a big breakfast was waiting, complete with fresh eggs and milk. A sort of relaxed feeling came over me as I lounged in a deep chair and held a one-way conversation on various subjects. I was feeling tired though, so I asked them if I could have a one-day grace in not mentioning Britain or having opinions. Then we talked of home and what had happened in the past two years. I wondered why Linda was so happy until I learned that my arrival was considered a great enough event for her to be excused from school that day! I'm glad I was of some value to someone!

For the next two weeks, I literally didn't have a spare moment. I went to the doctor to get a complete physical report. I visited oodles of friends, went to the beach, went to an airfield (a "postman's holiday"), slept, window shopped and also "ordinary" shopped, loafed, ate hugely, drove my car, talked, went to only three movies, and generally enjoyed myself.

Two days after I arrived, I went down to the beach for some sun. For some reason, the California sunshine decided to play tricks and refused to cooperate at all, with the result that I had to put on a sweater and finally go home cold. Naturally, I didn't tell my British friends about this until I could absorb their teasing. Later on I did get some very good sunshine and vigorous ocean bathing. The weather on the whole was partly cloudy but warm, which was the main point.

I spent most of my money on ice cream. I had it twice a day for eight days, rested for four days, and then had it at least once a day until I left. What a joy! Then too, my folks were trying to give me everything I wanted, so I had steak, chops, roasts, sweet potatoes, peas, string beans, lima beans, white flour rolls and biscuits, fruits, hot cakes, crisp bacon, eggs, milk, butter, and all the other things to make one's mouth water. Plenty of salad, lettuce and Thousand Island dressing. Ah, me! And no cabbage, no brussel sprouts, no Irish potatoes, no beets.

Have you in the States ever had to stop and think about how many coupons you might have had to spend on a dress, a coat, a suit, a shirt, stockings, socks, gloves, underwear, or even a tie if you were in Britain? I doubt it. Here you might find it difficult to procure your favorite article, but if you see something you like you can buy it. Your costs have gone up too, but nothing like they have in Britain. There you have a ration of 48 coupons a year. A coat takes 18 of those, a shirt about six, a pair of stockings or socks two, shoes from seven to nine, slippers three to five, a tie one, two to four handkerchiefs for one- which is about 40 coupons already, plus underwear, pajamas, dressing gown, extra pairs of shoes, socks, shirts, etc. When you must also buy some additional shirts, underwear, shoes, etc., the coupons disappear quite quickly. Not only that, but the rationing board may suddenly announce that new coupon books might not be released for an extra month or so, making the coupons stretch over a longer period. If you buy anything without coupons, the cost is prohibitive- for instance, hats. It is bad enough to have food on points, but on clothes too, the world of values becomes much more important.

Shopping at home was a great joy. No coupons. I didn't buy very much, as I didn't wear many civvies in Britain and I had plenty at home. What I did do was buy lots of little things to send to my friends in Britain. I spent a couple of nights with my stepmother packing and wrapping five-pound parcels. I was glad to be able to send them, knowing how they would be enjoyed. Scarves, socks, packages of noodle soup, dehydrated cranberry sauce, sweet potatoes, nail polish, compacts, powder, lipstick, soap, emery boards, and many other articles. Parcels like this would have been snubbed five years ago, but now every article was a special present. I had as much pleasure sending these as those girls did receiving them.

My first day of shopping was quite satisfactory, and when my father asked me what I bought, expecting me to say a coat, hat, dress, or suit, I surprised him enormously by throwing my hands together in great glee and answering, "Winter woolies." Ah yes, winter woolies (wonderful one-piece, long-sleeved, ankle-length, cotton-wool underwear), heavy socks, fur-lined shoes, and gloves! They simply couldn't believe it when I told them that I sometimes wore my heavy pajamas over winter woolies in bed, plus a sweater, a scarf, and socks, plus hugging two hot water bottles. I did it many times.

I didn't wear my uniform but three times at home. Once it worked for a serviceman's rate at a movie, which surprised me.

However, it was a pleasure to get out of uniform into loose light civvies. No strangers asked questions then, and I was glad of the rest.

In visiting my friends, though, naturally I was asked a thousand and two questions about my work and my experiences in Britain. First and foremost, they asked about the food situation. My answer was quite simple: Britain had the necessary food, but not in excess quantity, nor of much variety. Rations varied slightly according to availability of goods and were announced over the radio and in newspapers by government officials. Meat, butter, fats, bacon, eggs, cheese, tea, milk, preserves – were all strictly rationed per week, with a group of points for canned (tinned) goods. At Hamble, I gave my ration coupons to Mrs. Whitcomb to combine with the family's.

Usually there were few eggs, unless the billetor had children and was therefore allowed to keep chickens. Once I had one egg in three months; another time, I had three in four months. Since the Whitcombs had children, they were allowed to have chickens. So for the year I lived with them, I was privileged to have one egg for breakfast—as long as the chickens didn't go on strike, which they sometimes did.

Usually I had breakfast and dinner at the house (often alone at odd hours). The noon meal was at the ATA mess hall, or a bag lunch was prepared for me before I left. Most food was boiled, due to a lack of grease and oils. A beef roast on Sunday might be used in various ways until there was no more beef by Friday or Saturday.

There was one amusing incident regarding food. I had brought to England a can of popcorn kernels, to be popped whenever the time was ripe. I was invited to dinner where Edith, Kay, and Grace were staying, so I brought along the can and gave it to Mrs. Porter, their landlady. We waited a considerable time, and finally I went into the kitchen. There she was, standing patiently over the stove, trying to pop the kernels in boiling water! I found out later that they were used to caramel popcorn balls, or ready-made popcorn, with sugar yet, no salt!

The most horrible impression in the British food line appeared in the meat and fish shops. There was no refrigeration, no containers for the meat. It just hung unprotected from the rafters. Fish were even worse. They were tossed down on a big marble slab, open to the world of filth. No coverings for anything. It made you almost literally sick.

My friends asked about clothes, which I have already discussed. They questioned me about the weather, which was easy to answer – variable between bad and worse! They also wanted to know about the flying bomb damage.

I had seen quite a lot of bomb destruction. The area around St. Paul's was a vivid memory. Looking out the back of the American Red Cross Nurses' Club where I often stayed, you could see waste from the heavy bombs of 1941-1942. Wherever you walked, there were houses blasted and blocks deserted. Just walking along streets, you saw broken windows, gutted houses and churches, vacant lots.

I was in London the first night in June 1944 when the doodle-bugs, also called buzz-bombs or V-1s, came across. The alert went on just as I was getting into bed. About five minutes later I heard a terrific roar right over my head, causing me to duck involuntarily. "My goodness, that plane's flying awfully low," I thought. "Guess I'd better go downstairs." So I spent five hours downstairs, then finally went back up to bed, waking every two hours, not from the vibration of a bomb explosion but from the tremendous firing concussion of the rocket ack-ack guns nearby.

Can you imagine a bomb coming toward you, making a noise like a small airplane, getting closer and louder until your eyes almost pop out trying to see it? Your ears sort of stretch, trying to place the location. Then perhaps you hear the bomb overhead, and you can be 99 percent sure that you're safe. It's a great relief. But perhaps the noise stops before it gets to you. You duck into a shelter like a jackrabbit. The concussion of the explosion is like a vicious earthquake- sudden, jarring, violent. Many a time you are awakened at night just by the concussion alone, and it sends your heartbeat into an extremely rapid pace.

The jar is bad enough, but the worst effect of the flying bomb is its noise. Although it gives away its position, the steady putt-putt, reminding me of a Piper J-3 Cub, plays havoc with a person's nerves. You can hear the doodle-bugs for miles and wait for the tell-tale cut of the engine, which indicates the direct approach of destruction. You have absolutely no defense. When you had several hundred coming over during the day as well as at night- as they did from July to October- it was impossible to relax at all. Yet the people carried on as well as they could- joked and **ducked**.

While I was at home in September and October, the first rocket bombs (V-2s) appeared over England. When I returned, I heard my share. In one way they were not so bad, as they had no sound of approach. Thus when they hit, that was that, but they didn't affect thousands of others by their noise.

The British Sense of Humor

The British sense of humor is likely to arise at the most unusual times and often accompanies a great deal of patience. I've seen it in a railway carriage when the train stops on a siding for half an hour. Instead of griping seriously and cussing, as I've seen some very impatient Americans do, the British start joking about it. It passes the time and keeps others from getting too riled. They find a cheerful outlet for their emotions. The kidding comes rapidly and at the proper time to break the ice.

"Now what we are stopping for? Driver having his tea?" That's always the main excuse for anybody who isn't there.

"Probably forgot his sugar at the last station." says another.

"Well, I can see my girlfriend beating me over the head when I get in an hour late," remarks a Canadian lad.

"She should know by now that trains are always late."

"She wouldn't think of that. If I'm too late, maybe I can catch the 2:30 [it's 11:00 now] back home."

"At the rate we're going, you will be lucky to get into town, let alone out again."

"This was supposed to be a fast train," says another.

"I haven't decided whether it's a local or not yet," ventures an ATS private.

"Can't be a local. We skipped Eastleigh," says Canada.

"Oh," says a youngster, sticking his head out the window. "The engine has gone."

"Well, now we've had it!"

All this is accompanied by laughs and smiles, and nobody even thinks of getting serious over it, because it wouldn't do any good. There is no one to whom to complain and no alternative line to use, as there is no competing company. However, it would shame many impatient Americans to take such a tolerant attitude about some annoying incident like this.

But as to jokes, there are two disturbing factors. First, the British joke is based on their way of life and locale. That makes it difficult for others to understand. Their manner of telling the joke is different also. Secondly, I find many jokes have a nasty taste to them. Americans usually will classify their jokes according to the occasion and type of company. However, I have never heard so many "dirty" jokes as I've heard in theatres or by guests at parties in Britain. Clean jokes seem to be rare, but maybe that's due to the war, or else I have been in the wrong places!

Another question usually asked was about the attitude of the British towards the Americans. It was difficult to answer this, as each individual had his own impression. Just as we found certain people very friendly and helpful, so did we find many who took the Americans for all they could get and the devil take the hindmost. No doubt it was a great change for the complacent British to see all types of boys and girls from a country which they knew only from the movies. It was a surprising revelation to find that many British thought all people from Chicago were gangsters or tough in general; that everyone on a ranch always sang or had pistol fights; that Hollywood was a separate and distinct city. The movies had given them many erroneous conceptions, and it took a great deal of persuasion to convince them otherwise.

Some Americans, being away from home, thought they could do as they pleased and made a very bad impression by their attitude and behavior. Others, thank goodness, offset that impression by a friendly, tolerant attitude and good behavior. The Americans, always being in a hurry, were impatient with the slower British pace and lack of a multitude of things to do, and sometimes they became unnecessarily critical.

I must say that probably some of our American slang and terminology upset the British. We so often said "yeah" for "yes," and it took a while for them to realize that we weren't being rude. We were not so precise about our manners, and we were friendlier. To the Britisher who has always considered it "correct" to be introduced formally before starting a conversation, our approaches must have raised many eyebrows at first.

However, they're game. Alison, dear Alison, operations officer at Hamble, gave us a terrific jar one day. Kay Van D. and others were playing bridge on a particularly dull day, with Alison standing behind one of the players. Kay, trying to plan for the afternoon, asked Alison if she thought we would fly. Alison shook her head from side to side and uttered an affirmative "uh-huh." Kay and I both stared at her unbelievingly. Kay repeated the question and Alison did the same thing. We looked at each other and began to laugh. Poor Alison blushed mightily. She had heard us Americans uttering these peculiar grunts for answers so much that she decided that she might save some breath too. The negative headshake contradicted the affirmative sound, however, so we had to teach her the proper method. She had a stiff neck before long.

During my stay at home, I visited an old high school acquaintance who was in the WASPs (Women's Air Force Service Pilots). Dot Avery had started flying before me but had not been as fortunate in piling up hours, so she did not have the minimum of 300 hours to join the ATA. When the WASP began, however, she joined up and eventually passed through primary, basic, and advanced training, through B-25 school, to flying, as first pilot, a B-37 Ventura on low-target missions.

I went out to March Field near Riverside one evening with Dot and stayed over the next day. It was a grand day, over 100°F, and I simply absorbed all the heat I could and drank gallons of water. My arms turned brown for the first time in two years. What a marvelous feeling it was! And yet I met an American pilot in Scotland later, returning from hot and dusty Persia, and he was so glad to see Britain, with its coolness and greenness.

Dot didn't have a flight until the afternoon, so we hopped down to El Centro in a Vultee, BT-13. I took over in the air and map-read to our destination. I had to laugh at the navigation. We could see miles and miles – it was a gorgeous day, and way ahead there was a lake. Just one lake in the expanse of desert. That was lovely, as my course took me just to the right of it. So I sat and thought of England, with all its confusing and similar landmarks and no radio aids to guide me. Eastern states and the northwest are more similar to England geographically, I understand, but the desert waste east of Los Angeles was a cinch to navigate in good weather.

That evening a gang of us lounged in the living room of the barracks and gabbed. Here I found out some of the differences between the WASPs and the ATA. The girls were as interested in finding out about the ATA as I was in learning about them, so we had lots of fun. Some of them were anxious to know if they could join the ATA after the WASPs disbanded in December, 1944. I was not at all optimistic on that subject, as I knew that the ATA had already stopped training and was only giving conversions to a few ex-RAF fliers.

The subject of disbanding was the sad note in the conversation. Eight hundred to 1,000 well-trained women, many of whom wished to keep on flying in some capacity, were to be released to make room for returning operational pilots. I think that if the organization had been smaller and had not had so much adverse publicity attached to it, the girls might possibly have been kept on longer without any fuss. They were doing excellent work in many ways. They were flying low-target missions for the ack-ack batteries, not exactly a pleasant job. They were doing tracking and searchlight missions, simulated strafing, smoke laying. They were doing weather observations for the benefit of all who flew and special hush-hush radio control work with small planes, experimental work that might in the future revolutionize certain sorts of flights. They were test pilots at factories. They were ferry pilots, flying everything from Cubs to B-29 Super-fortresses.

Most of them ferried only single-engine machines, since the male pilots wanted and received most of the twin-engine and four-engine deliveries. What they flew depended mainly on the commanding officer. If the C.O. disliked women pilots, they only received the so-called simpler jobs, usually the worst, or only flew as co-pilots with male first pilots. If the C.O. had no prejudice, he usually gave the girls equal jobs with the men. The latter group showed that they could do the job, and the C.O. was proud of them.

At March Field, the girls flew as pilots and co-pilots on tow-target missions with B-26 Marauders, considered one of the hottest ships in the world, and as first pilots on B-37 Venturas, not flown without a lot of due respect by both sexes. There were many other special jobs the women fliers did too, including chauffeuring high-ranking officials around; instructing in all phases of flying, including instrument work; and other odd jobs.

The ATA was different in that everyone was in the ferrying end only, each flew as the PIC (pilot in command), the girls flew everything on an equal basis with the men- they were not restricted in any way. Also, the women in the ATA comprise about one-tenth of the total. If they were to be disbanded, two stations would have to be closed down, as they were composed entirely of women- with women C.O.s, adjutants, etc.- and two other stations would have to be cut by about one third their strength. The women are mixed with the men so much that they are taken for granted and are an integral part of the organization.

Both the WASPs and I got a kick out of some of the comparisons. For instance, they liked my uniform, especially the forage hat (side cap) better than theirs, while I liked their nifty attire. Some of them liked my gold-braid ATA wings better than their metal ones, while I thought theirs looked sharper. They liked the idea of ATA rank, which made us look like officers at least. It always seems that we like somebody else's things better than that which we have ourselves, doesn't it? They thought that ATA ferrying would be tops and while I agreed with them to a certain extent, I tried to disillusion them. ATA ferrying at times is absolute hell.

The WASPs had no insurance. This, I thought, was about the highest sort of crime. They were risking their lives as much as other fliers, but since they were civilians they were not permitted to receive

Army or Air Force insurance. No company would give the girls insurance as a group, and individually it was too high for a girl to pay. ATA pilots and flight engineers are covered as a group for death, loss of limbs, or eyes – and they are civilians too. In fact, as each year passed the company reduced the rates because of the few accidents. The ATA organization, not the individual pilots, pays the insurance. Also, we receive good medical care and hospitalization free.

The girls at March Field lived in wooden barracks, without any decorations except as the individual girls wished to liven it up. ATA members are dispersed into various private billets in nearby towns. The billeting situation is rather difficult, but it is amazing how well the British people take in strangers. Of course in many instances they are required to do so, but the ATA does not hold to compulsory billeting. We are given a subsistence allowance with which to pay our living expenses. The WASPs' room and board was included in their pay.

March Field is an enormous place and is considered one of the best fields in the States. It has all facilities including, to my delight, a soda fountain, where I indulged in giant milkshakes and hamburgers. British airfields as a whole are not so large but are well-dispersed, with all sorts of cold Nissen huts. Many times at British aerodromes I have walked 15 minutes to get to the mess hall for breakfast or dinner from the women's sleeping quarters. When it is raining, it is very uncomfortable. The girls in the WASPs were allowed to have cars and thus were able to get around the field without much difficulty. Also, there were well-paved roads and sidewalks, so one was able to keep from getting too muddy even if one did walk.

The WASPs had to report for duty at 8:00 AM and on special missions even earlier. ATA never started until 9:00 or 9:30 AM (sunrise). Also, the WASPs flew night missions, while the ATA always had to be down on the ground a quarter of an hour before sunset, called "last landing time." In winter time, that meant around 4:30 in the afternoon, but in the summer we sometimes flew as late as 10:00 or 10:30 at night. Sometimes we would wait around until 5:00 PM in the summer and then be given two priority chits to complete before 10:00 PM.

WASPs flew on instruments and had radio, although they seldom went up under instrument conditions if it could be avoided. Since ATA flying was supposed to be done under visual contact conditions, there were many inactive days. Contact minima in the ATA are about the same as the USA instrument minima – 2,000 yards visibility and a 800-foot ceiling. With the ever-changing British weather, it meant that pilots must be continually on the alert for bad conditions and effect a safe landing before being caught under instrument conditions.

The WASPs flew more hours, due to longer trips such as three-hour tow-target missions and 1,000-2,000-mile ferrying jobs. The ATA gave little chance to pile up hours, 20 per month being fair, 30 per month good, and 40 per month exceptional. Very seldom did we fly over one- or two-hour jaunts, due to the size of the country. A trip of 400 miles from Prestwick, Scotland, to the southern coast near Southampton is about the same as a trip from Los Angeles to San Francisco. To us, a 400-mile trip is very long.

But the ATA did give us a chance to make many takeoffs and landings and to fly many different types of aircraft. During one month I flew 18 various types of aircraft, which is more than some pilots have flown in a lifetime. My Spitfire deliveries totaled one for each half hour, which is good practice on "circuit and bumps." I consider an hour of experience in taking off, landing, map reading, and flying while dodging the weather and balloon barrages and artillery ranges without instrument or radio aids equal to any single three-hour jaunt in the USA.

The WASP's training was different than the ATA's. The WASPs went through the same basic training as army cadets, except for gunnery, advanced aerobatics, and formation flying. They had primary, basic, and advanced training, with some light twin-engine work plus instrument and radio practice, as well as ground school, which consisted of navigation, meteorology, code, military courtesy, drill, etc., etc. Then some went to single-engine ferrying, or to twin-engine advanced training, or to some other specialized job. Eventually they ended up in a particular job with little likelihood of much variety or change. I know I should have liked to have had the WASP training with its precision and instrument training, yet many WASPs would have liked to have logged some of my aircraft types.

The ATA, although a civilian organization, had uniforms and officers' ranks. But thankfully we did not have to do any marching or programmed exercises! We finally did have to learn to salute, as we had to do when Mrs. Roosevelt, Mrs. Churchill, and Mrs. Hobby came to visit.

I visited Dot again two weeks later. It was only 85-90 degrees, but since I had absorbed enough heat by then, I felt as "washed out" as the rest and drank gallons of water. Brownie, a friend of Dot's, took me up in a Beechcraft C-45, which I flew for a while. It is amazing how rough one gets for lack of practice! But, as usual, it was fun. I guess I'll never grow tired of flying. It's too fascinating!

Aside from visiting my friends, sleeping, eating, and shopping, I did very little. Ever since I was a youngster, though, I've liked to keep scrapbooks. In my teens, it was on auto racing, which I followed with great zeal. This time I found a gorgeous, huge book, about two by two and a half feet (yes, feet!), into which I pasted oodles of pictures of aircraft. I found small shots of my old light planes – Cubs, Luscombes, Taylorcraft, Waco, etc. – which I entered first, along with some snapshots of me and my instructor at Oakland in 1940, those proud days pre- and post-solo. Then from *Flying, Air News, Aeroplane, Flight,* and other magazines, I collected and pasted in all the planes I had flown in the ATA in order in which I flew them. Just to make everything colorful, I drew lines around them with colored lead pencils. When I return home for good, I shall finish my ATA section and continue with a third section of miscellaneous pictures. I shall then have something to remind me of one of the most interesting periods of my life.

Contact! Britain!

XII.

THEY JUST DON'T UNDERSTAND

Generally, I felt ill at ease at home. Outwardly there was no recognition that a war was being fought; people griped at little things, which showed they didn't know how lucky they were; inwardly people realized there was a war progressing but had no idea just what it was all about. They had no buzz-bombs or rocket bombs to upset them, they had few frontline soldiers milling about to give them the real facts (the boys would rather not talk anyhow), there was the feeling of almost certain ocean protection (except for rumors of ocean-spanning rockets and the actual Jap balloons, which came later), there was the atmosphere of plenty despite rationing (and they griped more over their rationing than the British did, who seldom had even any of the unrationed goods of America). They showed little interest in uniforms generally, seemingly taking them for granted.

Yet it was nice to be able to find in the USA certain foods unobtainable in Britain, to shop without coupons, to read through 36 pages of newspapers, although they seldom said more than the

British four-pager. It was good to know that America still had something at home to make one forget Britain or any other place. It was good to drive one's own car, to pull up to drive-ins; it was grand just to be home and forget.

But after a week or two, my conscience pricked me. I wasn't fighting an actual war, but I was doing a darn sight more in Britain than most of the fancy dressed gals swaggering down the street. There was nothing at home for me to do equal to that work, so I wanted to get back. Yes, I was willing to go back to the tight-cropped British with all their so-called idiosyncrasies (to us) in order to keep on flying and to be near the front where I could be of some benefit. There are so many boys who expressed the same desire after a home furlough, and nobody but those overseas can explain it.

The British people had been through so much, and we were just happy to be able to contribute to the war effort in the best way we knew, which was flying. The ATA motto, in Latin "*Aetheris Avidi*," was "Eager for the Air." I am sure that "eager to help" was an attitude shared by all the pilots during those terrible years.

On the train to Chicago, I met an ETO (European Theatre of Operations) navigator home on leave. We had some enjoyable discussions, which excluded other passengers. One day in Wyoming, we picked up a newspaper and ran through 36 pages trying to find out what was happening in Europe. On one of the middle pages in the first section, buried half way down the column, was a four-inch article saying that bombers had been over Germany, England had buzz-bombs, and a few other items. On the front page were several articles on the Pacific war, with even less actual news. Strange that the major European war going on in such great strength should have only four inches of news that didn't even tell how the actual lines were progressing. We looked at each other and said,

"No wonder they don't know what's going on – and don't care!" When the war is over, the atmosphere will be different, and yet there will always be a slight breach between those at home and those who were overseas.

I arrived at Chicago after a pleasant, fast train ride (unlike British service); my cousins met me, but I didn't have much time before shipping out on the evening plane for New York. Approaching the latter at night was a grand sight. The night was clear, and looking out over the starlit city, the jewels of all the city's lights glittered splendidly. You could tell that the air was crisp. The lights were like a cluster of stars, dazzling in their beauty. It was the first time I had seen a large city at night from the air. I want to see it and many others again. When I return, I want to fly at night between two skies of brilliant diamonds.

Contact! Britain!

XIII.

WHAT A SMALL WORLD

Montreal once again! After two years I was back to that airfield where I had puttered around in an AT-6 for my ATA check. There was little delay this time, though. In four days I was off in a B-24 Liberator with Squadron Leader Anderson of the RAFTC (Royal Air Force Transport Command) at the controls. The day before we left, I bought oodles of bananas, grapefruit, oranges and lemons to take to my friends. I also found some Calobar sun glasses and some wool-lined shoes, which were impossible to purchase in the States. Canada seemed to have most everything.

The weather was bad over the northern route, so we flew six hours south to Bermuda. It was a lovely trip, clear all the way, with Bermuda shining brilliantly in the sun as we neared it. Such a small place, I thought, a string of islands with a big airfield on one flat side. So very easy to miss in bad weather. Our radio operator was having some trouble, but fortunately the navigator was on the ball. I stood behind the pilot and co-pilot as they circled and brought the huge machine down to mother earth. Little Andy, only about 5'6", dispelled the rumor that B-24 pilots must be big and strong. He handled the aircraft deftly and did a beautiful smooth landing – as he did on all three of his landings.

We had passed Maine, Boston, and New York and covered a lot of ocean down to that pinpoint. Somehow it almost seemed routine. The flight engineer flitted between the cabin and the rear of the ship to check the fuel. The radio operator searched frantically for an important little slip of paper, which he never did find until after we landed. The navigator stayed down in the nose nearly all the time. I wedged up against the door between the cabin and bomb-bay, as the radar equipment, Mae Wests and dinghies took up the rest of the room – and there was very little. The engines purred steadily and "George," the automatic pilot, kept us on our path.

In Montreal I had needed to put on my coat for the first time since leaving England. In Bermuda, it was warm again and fresh and invigorating. We lunched in the mess, having steaks and ice cream. Suddenly, there was a tap on my shoulder.

"Well, for heaven's sake, where did you come from?" I exclaimed.

"I've done one trip to Prestwick and am now on my way across to India," said the pilot. It was one of the RAFTC personnel who had traveled to the States with me on the Queen Elizabeth six weeks previously.

We planned to take off at around 6:00 PM so that we could fly through the night and land at the Azores early in the morning. Unfortunately, the number three engine acted up and we couldn't get off. In a way, that was fine. We were all tired, and Bermuda was a dry, pleasant climate. We had drinks (me, my coca-cola) in the officer's club and then slept until noon. That night we did get away and started on an uncomfortable, monotonous journey to the Azores.

It was long – eleven hours. It was cold midship without any heating. I was dressed in my RAF sitcot back in the bomb area with an oxygen mask at 20,000 feet for two hours – and I was cold! But it was hot in the radio compartment when I could be there—hot and stuffy and close. It was most uncomfortable because I had to keep moving so that the flight engineer could get aft to check the transfer of fuel. It was very monotonous and boring as we sailed along, the four engines droning in the still night. A cloud layer covered the sky, and at 9,000 feet we couldn't make out the ocean. So we just roared blindly across the miles of water.

We came to the Azores on top of broken clouds, using the radio beam. Andy let down on the south side, contact, and as we made a wide descending glide, the airfield appeared. What a huge place it was! There was a runway under construction, a tremendously long one. We landed next to it, in what appeared to be a short run compared to the new one. Much to my surprise, we pulled up in about half the distance without undue haste. It was already hot at 8:00 AM. At 9:00 AM, sitting in the mess, I met another pilot friend from the group on the Queen Elizabeth. He was returning from India.

We went into the RAF section and tried to eat breakfast. Never have I seen such unappetizing food. The tents and huts looked dirty, and we felt sorry for the British men who were stationed there. I didn't see the American side, as we were only there a couple of hours for refueling; then we began the third and last lap to Scotland.

The last lap consisted of being hungry, having the coffee go cold on us, and being extremely sleepy. I had to slip back in the rear of the plane several times to use the "john"- that is, a little tin can. When we had checked in Montreal, the navigator found there was no large container in the rear as usual, so I brought a small tin can, the only thing I could find. It was difficult to use it normally, but when I had on my oxygen mask and then had to strip off my sitcot-ah me! how very awkward and uncomfortable. And it was so cold out too!

For some reason the weather in the British Isles was grand. Over Northern Ireland I could map read from the reflection of rivers, streams, lakes, railways, and roads. The moon shone brightly. I saw Turnberry lighthouse and the coast of Ayrshire twenty miles away. I listened in as we rode the "beam." There was still a blackout imposed, although a few dim streetlights were allowed. I couldn't make out the Prestwick aerodrome until we were practically over it. The lights on either side of the long runway lit up the landing path. With a slight cross-wind we drifted a bit, but corrected and made a nice landing. I kept thinking, "Now we can't crash here; we've just come across the ocean and we can't prang at the end of so many thousands of miles!"

We didn't prang, but another serious situation developed. I almost didn't make it through Customs. Trying to be helpful, I had brought the little can off the airplane with me to empty into a suitable site. Bad idea!

The Customs officials stopped me, suspecting that I was trying to bring in something illegal. This caused considerable consternation, with many questions and much delay. I even offered to give the can to the officials, but they wouldn't take it. Actually, they stepped away. Red-faced, I finally told them the whole story, with much laughter from nearby pilots and crews. It was one of the most embarrassing moments of my life, standing there holding a can of urine!

When I finally passed through Customs, etc., and walked out into the reception center, whom should I run into but Jim Usher, a radio operator, one more of the Queen Elizabeth ferry group. I had seen one at Montreal, several at Bermuda, one at the Azores even with only a two-hour stop, and then the final welcome by Jim at the termination of such a long trip. Yes, what a small world!

Well, I had had that trans-oceanic plane trip anyhow. It is something to remember, because there are still relatively few who have had the experience. Also, it makes you think of Lindbergh, Corrigan, and others who, in small horsepower single-engine machines, crossed all that water so many years before. It seems impossible that they could have done it. What courage, or perhaps what foolishness, inspired it! Yet it stirs one's imagination to think of those people in the pioneering days who risked their lives to make history so that others would try to improve on their methods and records and, by so doing, open up vast airways to bring the world closer together.

The next day I went down south to report for a flight check. I stayed in London, but the following morning I woke up with a terrific cold. As usual it went into a heavy catarrhal condition, which lasted for several weeks. About the third week, severe pains developed in my abdomen, and I shot out to the Canadian hospital. Instead of being appendicitis as feared, it turned out that I had coughed so much and so hard I had strained all those muscles. 'Twasn't no fun neither!

Contact! Britain!

XIV.

JOLLY OL' ENGLAND

In December 1944, I finally had a check flight in an Albemarle, a British tricycle glider-towing twin-engine plane, and returned to Prestwick for duty. It was getting a bit cold those days, but nothing compared to several weeks in January. I was comfortable wearing my winter woolies and greatcoat, in addition to the usual.

It took a long time for me to get a chit for a B-25 Mitchell, but it finally came just after Christmas. Ah me, what a nice plane! Poor Davies – he was the flight engineer and disliked intensely the idea of flying a "first" trip (a "nursing trip," they called it) with a woman. I really didn't blame him. He just moaned, "What have I done to deserve this?" I answered, "Probably a lot."

It was an uneventful trip of 45 minutes, practically a long journey for Britain. The landing gear with the nose wheel was so firm and solid. On the takeoff it felt like two takeoffs, one when the nose wheel cleared the ground and again when the whole aircraft slid into the air. Then when everything was adjusted, Davies took over for his fun while I played with the radio. Coming into land at KB on the long runway, I was surprised at the flat angle of glide and didn't touch down until the middle of the runway. There was still plenty of room, however. I just couldn't believe that she possessed such marvelous handling characteristics on the approach. It was difficult to lose speed even when the wheels were down and, with the tricycle gear, full flaps could be used in almost any wind. Yet when she sat down she stayed and slowed up quickly without vicious use of brakes. Yes the B-25 became one of my favorites.

On one very breezy day, operations gave me a "Wildcat," a Grumman F4F, one of the US navy carrier fighters. The very narrow undercart with a mid-wing makes it rather unstable directionally, and special care has to be taken on cross-wind landings. I took off without any trouble, rather amazed at its short run, although the wind was quite strong. I started winding up the wheels but found the lever too stiff, so I adjusted everything for cruising and trimmed for hands off. Then I took both hands and my right leg and managed to roll it up the rest of the way. So awkward. I suppose it saves a great deal of weight by not having a hydraulic system, but I'd much rather just pull a lever and have "Mr. Joe Gremlin" whip the wheels up.

In the air I thought the Wildcat flew beautifully. In fact, it was one of the lightest and smoothest on controls that I have flown. I rather prefer it in the air to its big brother, the F6F Hellcat, because of its lightness, which allows it to respond extremely well, and the fact that I felt right at home in its small cockpit. In landing, I found the runway at my particular airfield "out of wind" (cross-wind), and blowing up to 35 miles per hour. Being my first trip in one, I decided to land on a nearby airfield where the runway was directly into the wind. This I did using no flaps at all, and she sat down like a peach. It was one of those landings which you always hope for but seldom make, one where the roll-on is so smooth that you are not sure you are down.

Another new type of plane came in January during some terrible blizzards. The snow storms were rather frequent, but since I wanted to fly the Dominie, a small twin-engine plane, I took off and started dodging the storms. The Dominie is an amazing aircraft. It is a bi-plane of equal spans, with two 200 horsepower in-line Gipsy Queen engines in the lower wings. The pilot sits dead center, right up in the pointed nose, while there are seats for five or six passengers in the fuselage.

This Dominie (Rapide or Dragon-Rapide) has been one of Britain's foremost passenger planes for a good many years. Even today in late 1945, despite its slow cruising speed of 125 mph, it continues to fly the domestic airlines around the United Kingdom. It can take off and land within such a short space that one wouldn't believe it unless one saw it done. On one engine it performs smoothly and safely, even with a full load. It will maintain height on one engine at 85 mph, will climb at 80 with a full load, and has a single-engine ceiling of 3,100 feet. For Britain, with its few mountains, that is sufficient. It used to, and still does, land in small green pastures on the many islands off the mainland; it will take in almost any cross-wind, despite its bi-plane structure. The wheels do not retract, the props are fixed pitch, so there is very little to go wrong. It would be a fairly nice ship for a private owner in the States, with easy maintenance, excellent performance, and good economy (it uses very little gasoline).

My experience with the Dominie was one of those where I wonder why something serious didn't happen. When I took off after one snow storm, I bucked about a 40-mph gusty wind for about an hour. I saw another storm approaching, so I attempted to get around it. Unfortunately, these storms were running together more, so that I couldn't find a hole. I crept along over HX, an airfield, and glanced down to notice which way they were landing. Then I looked up to see the storm rushing at me. At the far upwind end of the field, at about 800 feet, I turned sharply to port, closed the throttles,

157

and made a close U approach onto the runway in use. That approach didn't take more than one minute, probably less. As I was still about 400 feet up, about half a mile away from the field, I saw the snow begin to fall on the far end of the runway. The rest of the approach was a race between my getting down before the blizzard enveloped the whole runway. I was a bit amused but not frightened, because the weather was still good behind me and I knew another airfield nearby which was still in the clear. However, I was challenged by this blizzard, so I headed in to see if I could beat it—a poor decision on my part.

As I came in, I could see the snow fluttering in just as if a window shade was being drawn about every 50 feet. I touched down at the beginning of the runway in the clear and rolled to the intersection half way down, where I met the blizzard. As soon as I hit it, my visibility was cut from about 6 miles to about 50 yards, and then to about 10 feet. I turned off at the intersection and faced into the wind, as the Dominie won't behave in a strong wind and I couldn't see a thing anyhow. I kept the engines running as a matter of control and just sat.

Nobody will believe it but I sat there for exactly 27 minutes while the snow whipped against the windscreen and formed on the wings. At the end of that time, I could see about 50 feet again, and suddenly there appeared a fire truck, grinding to a jarring halt about 10 feet short of the starboard wing-tip. The fireman got into the Dominie.

"Are you all right?" he asked.

"Perfectly," I answered, "But this wind is too strong for me to taxi, so I'll have to wait until the storm blows over."

"OK. We wondered where you were. We saw you roll into the storm, and we've been wandering around ever since trying to find you."

I finally taxied it in slowly, with some men holding on to the wingtips.

I can't pass up telling about one of the most amusing, and to me satisfying, experiences. This is primarily for women pilots, but I think everyone will enjoy it and understand the feelings of the young man in the story. It was during a Spitfire flight at about 2,000 feet on one of those unusually fairly clear days. Suddenly I was aware of a plane at my side, an American P-51 with US markings. I could see the pilot quite clearly, as he was that close. He made overtures and signs with his hands to instigate a little dogfight. I shook my head "no" twice, both because I was not too proficient in aerobatics and also had an overnight bag at my side, which would fly all over the place.

Then I had a bright idea. I took off my leather helmet and goggles, shook my hair, and blew him a kiss with my hand. The expression on his face was one for the ages. His hand flew up against his head, and you could see the "Oh no!" expression—then he peeled off into a sharp right turn and disappeared. I just had to grin—and wondered what he said, or if he said anything, to his pals that night.

Christmas and New Year's of 1944 passed quietly. The most important event was a special turkey dinner at the Craig's, where Vera Strodl lived. There was the most luscious turkey and stuffing and, strange to Americans, plenty of sausages. They had no cranberry sauce however, had never heard of it used with such dinners. For one who thinks the British can't cook, here was proof that one was wrong. The little pom-poms, I call them, for dessert, a sort of sugared meringue – mmmmm! On December 28th they had another turkey for New Year's celebration, as the Craig's daughter in the ATS was having a 24-hour pass. So that made two turkey dinners in five days. Yep, that was okay.

As for New Year's Eve itself, I found myself stuck out at Bristol after delivering a plane. I went to the American Red Cross, read, and slept in the lounge. At about 10:45 I fell fast asleep as a doctor and an engineer nearby had a vigorous discussion. At 11:50 I awakened; at 12:00 we said "Happy New Year" to each other, shook hands, and went to our respective beds. A very quiet evening, a very lonely one compared to what we might have had in the States, but a much more comfortable one than the front-line boys were having.

In January 1945, we had two bad spells of weather in Scotland—one of eleven days of continuous "washout" and another of ten days—which extended into February. My winter woolies stayed on even at night, plus my heavy pajamas and a sweater, a hot water bottle, and an electric stove if possible. I didn't think it was so bad as in England though, not so damp. In fact, as we checked the maps each morning, we were amazed to find that the temperature in Yorkshire (east England) and the Midlands and south were five to 20 degrees **colder** than Scotland and that the warmest place was off the northwest tip of Scotland in the Hebrides! It just didn't seem right, but there it was!

Up at Prestwick the Americans bustled around the airfield amidst all the RAF and ATA. There was an American officer's mess called "Adamton House" on the east side of the field in a small woods. Most of the Americans ate there, and many transients lived upstairs. I sometimes had lunch and dinner there, for it was by far the best food obtainable. Fruits, fruit juices, and vegetables made all the difference, plus GI cooking so that everything tasted different and better. We also had access at times to the Post Exchange, the good old "PX," which furnished a bit of the USA in the way of cigarettes, candy bars, soap, and other odds and ends.

Here too we met many pilots, navigators, colonels, lieutenants, Navy personnel, infantry, artillery, signal corps, ATC captains, and other officers. We would see a person one night, and the next day he would be on his way home by air. Their eyes would be shining so brightly, knowing that soon they would be winging their way to New York or Washington. The transatlantic pilots would converse about India, North Africa, Bermuda, Azores, South America, Iceland,

Greenland, and other points without a flicker of their eyelids. The world became intimate and close.

One day I saw a familiar face. I couldn't recall the name, but I was sure he had worked for West Moreau, my first instructor, at Oakland. We eyed each other warily and then finally spoke. Captain Wells of the ATC, with three broad rings on his sleeve, had taught a group of CPT students at the same time that I was plugging along with West in the 50-hp Cub. At that time he was on loan from United Air Lines before going on duty as a co-pilot. Now he was a senior captain of a C-54, and he seemed to enjoy it greatly. Naturally we gabbed in order to find out any news of the old crowd. That's how it always is when old friends meet.

Of course, there was the argument in the ATA about having instrument time. The ATA said "No" and discouraged any attempt at Link practice or flying through bad weather. They figured that just a little time would be detrimental and cause the pilot to go beyond his capabilities. In many cases there were no radios in planes and in ferrying, there were no radio crystals, as the factories, MUs (maintenance units), and squadrons kept their own. If no radio, no instrument work, said the ATA. Sound advice, certainly. But ATA could have authorized a complete instrument and radio course of about two to three weeks during their training and insisted upon complete radio equipment in planes. It was the only organization in the UK without radio. On washout days, the Link Trainer could have been used to improve technique and avoid the terrible waste of time that unflyable days provided.

When the ATA first started, the pilots, without much training at all, simply jumped in and flew planes from A to B as quickly as possible. The years 1940 and 1941 were ones of action, not training. As the personnel grew more numerous and training became more thorough, a good instrument course could have been made available, though. But by this time the ATA had decided the pilots had done a good enough job under visual-contact conditions and did not want to spend any more money than necessary, especially with the red tape it would have taken to have fully equipped radios in all planes. So we had no instrument or radio training. Any that we did get was by our own hook.

I managed to get in four and a half hours under the hood of the twin-engine Oxford with the C.O. of an RAF instrument flight school. He was swell, and due to his calmness and instruction during those first few difficult hours, I gained confidence which kept me from panic during some tough weather conditions. In three years of British weather, despite all the care you might take, you are bound to run into sudden, unavoidable bad weather. Thanks to Flight Lt. Sims, I managed to fly safely through those difficulties.

After those four and a half hours, I got an hour in the back of an AT-6 Harvard with Vera as safety pilot and a couple of hours on the basic instruments in a Fairchild 24 with safety pilots. Sometimes I would practice on various aircraft and actually go through some cloud from which I knew I could recover. Many were the times when the haze reduced visibility to a mile, and instead of straining my eyes, I scanned the instruments.

The British seldom gave any encouragement for anything, but the good old Americans were still in there and trying to help when they possibly could. The RAF at Prestwick would not allow us to use their Link Trainer, but I took some time from Sgt. "Ken" and Sgt. "Sax" on the American side. They were great. By the time I left there I had a total of 35 hours of Link under my belt, enough of a basis for that instrument rating I want when I return to the States. At some of the RAF stations where I was stuck, the sergeants there would be glad to give me an hour or so, which restored some of my faith in the British.

One day in March, I received an issue of the *Air Facts* magazine, to which I had subscribed. In it was an article about the Gumman Widgeon- what it looked like inside, the position of the controls, and how it handled in taxiing, taking off, climbing, cruising, on one engine, approaching and landing both on land and water, etc. I found it very interesting, as I like to know what a plane feels like. Then I, in a great brainstorm, thought I should do something similar on the Spitfire, as so many Americans had asked about its flying characteristics. So I wrote out a description on a couple of washout mornings and sent it to *Air Facts* – and promptly forgot all about it.

In April, much to my amazement, I received a nice letter from Mr. Collins, editor, with a check. I nearly fainted with joy and surprise. I had done it for fun, and here it had bounced into a profitable article in an established magazine. It was too much for me, so I sent the check very quick-like to my bank and wandered around in a cloud the rest of the day. First I knew that it had been published was in June when I received a letter from Helen Richey, ex-ATA, who said she had seen it in the May 1945 issue. When I eventually received my copy, naturally I pored over it with great pride. My first published article! Ah me! I was quite happy.

During April, we all wondered how the Germans kept on fighting and when they would give up. A few false rumors stirred us, and since usually that happens before the real thing, we figured it would be very soon. It was the slowness of an actual clear-cut declaration that made V-E day less important than it otherwise would have been. Sections seemed to surrender, but there was no official termination until the Big Three made their speeches. Many went to work on V-E Day, May 6th, not having heard Churchill's announcement, but they soon fell into the swing of things.

At Prestwick itself, it was fairly quiet. I was rather glad I wasn't in a big mass of humanity in Glasgow or London. Glasgow, I understand, had many pubs and stores pilfered the evening before V-E Day. Prestwick had its celebration at the "Cross," where more people congregated than I knew existed in that town. There was cheering and dancing and smiles spread over all faces.

The Americans there did little celebrating though, because as most of them said to me, "This war isn't over yet. I'm not through and going home. I am glad that this one part is over; now we can concentrate on the Japs. But I haven't a feeling of great joy. There's still too much to be done yet." So a group of us went out and played volleyball at the American Red Cross Club. A few got drunk in town. It was just a sort of an anti-climax, for the European war had been over days ago. But there was no doubt that inside we heaved a sigh of relief.

XV.

TRAVELING IS EDUCATION

I had a good time at Prestwick, but when I heard that certain women from three pools were permitted to ferry across to the continent, I immediately applied for a transfer. This came through, and I reported to Aston Down, near Stroud and Bristol in southern England, on May 24, 1945. I arrived in great style in an Anson-loaded down with three suitcases, a kit bag, an overnight bag, a bicycle, and a passenger- at 9:45 PM, just before sunset. What a journey! Since there was no plane directly from Prestwick, after lunch they gave me an Oxford up to Lossiemouth, in the north of Scotland, one hour and 40 minutes from Prestwick. There I picked up an Anson and flew it back five hours to Aston Down. Yes, it was a bit tiring.

Ann Blackwell had been posted there too, arriving before me. We had rooms in the same house in Cirencester, about ten miles from the airfield. Luckily, Ann had a car for transportation. It was at this billet that I had the most comfortable bed I ever had in

Britain. It had a lovely thick innerspring mattress, which refused to sag in the middle and curved in the right places.

We had a country fair in Cirencester one week. Ann, Mrs. Lush, and I threw dozens of darts in order to win some of the blue and pink plates, cups, and saucers, etc. I immediately tossed three darts into three different playing cards on the wall and won a large scrubbing brush, which Ann kept for me. After a while we found it had been stolen or lost, so Ann went back and promptly won another one. We also won several plates, salt shakers, ash trays, and glasses and enjoyed ourselves on the merry-go-round and other concessions. We had fun, despite the six-pences we shelled out!

As the European war had finished when we arrived at Aston Down, there were very few jobs going to the continent. We took our typhoid and other shots and did our VHF (very high frequency) radio course and a bit of flying. The radio course was granted to those doing continental ferrying, to be used only in case of emergency. Ann and I did several "homing" runs, which consisted of our calling up a station and asking for a homing or course to steer in order to get to the particular airfield. All we did was to steer the course given us. With this VHF system, instead of the pilot doing the orientation, the ground stations did it, leaving the pilot to concentrate on other things.

My first trip to Europe was as a stooge in an Anson to a little field in the northwest of Belgium. We had to fly to the Straits of Dover and cross the channel at that point. The pilot purposely went to Calais to show me the damage, and then we followed the coast to our destination, circling over Holland to say that we had been over it. As we left Dover, the weather was perfect, and Calais on the other end of the 22 miles seemed quite close. I looked back at those "white cliffs of Dover," and I must say they looked pretty good. They were not white—rather, a sort of dirty gray—but in contrast to the green slopes adjoining, they were outstanding. To the British, they are a symbol of England, just as the Statue of Liberty is to America.

166

Then, looking forward again, I saw Griz-Nez, a small point with a gray cliff similar to the Dover cliffs just north of it, presenting another good landmark. It seemed strange that as we approached Griz-Nez and Calais, we were touching the western part of a huge piece of land, with a great many millions of people, scoured by war. The huge guns on a small area of sand at Pas de Calais were blown up by bombing, and the bomb craters were evenly distributed over several square miles to break up any equipment. That was the first sign I saw of damage. Calais itself didn't seem to be badly bombed, although the harbor installations and some of the military houses were destroyed. Several airfields we passed were covered by fill-in craters. Some of the fields had only a short concrete runway with about a dozen dispersal or parking circles for aircraft.

In one section, we noticed a large lake, but upon closer inspection we realized that it was an overflooding of land from the breaking of dikes. Some trees jutted out from the water, and a few house tops were discernable. A few fences just barely showed on the high ground. It would take months and months for it to drain away.

We approached our destination and landed on the short Sommerfield wire track which served as the runway. A British RAF duty crew met us and took us in a jeep to the flying control in a stone building. We found out that the Germans had used the field for mining practice (and not coal mining!), and over 9,000 mines had been taken from the runways, perimeter tracks, and buildings. Some of the field was still mined. In fact when Captain Bayly arrived, he stepped over a fence to pluck some flowers. An RAF corporal yelled out to him, "I say, sir, you'd better come back. That area's still mined." Needless to say, Big Bill scampered back on his tip-toes but fast!

Soft Landings

A "Sommerfield" track was a heavy-gauge wire-mesh reinforcement that could be lifted and moved. Used to cover grass surfaces at temporary advanced airfields, it provided less drag on takeoffs and hopefully made for smoother landings. It was used by many squadrons on the south coast of the UK preparatory to D-Day buildup. The US Air Force used perforated steel sheets, with rolled ends and holes about one foot or more in diameter and whose planks locked together. These were generally known at "PSP": pieced steel planking. Because they had a springy flexibility, they could make your landings, at times, unpredictable and exciting.

We went into the small town to a hotel requisitioned by the British. Dinner was quite good, served by French waitresses. We window-shopped a bit, but the prices were so high and the quality of the goods so poor that we just looked. As I walked down the street ahead of my companions, who had stopped at one shop, a little tow-headed boy about five years old, with two front teeth missing, smiled broadly at me and said something, probably "hello" in Dutch. I was rather startled, but his little face absolutely glowing with happiness and a grin literally spreading from ear to ear prompted me into cheerfully saying "hello." He and his big sister walked on rather reluctantly, and I turned to continue my "shopping."

As I hesitated, a couple of seconds later before reaching a shop, the sound of running feet made me look up. Here was the little tow-head, grin big as ever, skidding up to me and stuttering out an uncertain "hel-hello," with pride written all over his countenance. I just ached to take the little darling into my arms and give him a big hug. I managed to say "hello" again, just as his mother called to him.

He turned slowly, and I said "goodbye." From the solemn expression which appeared when his mother called, his face suddenly changed back into that terrific smile. He exploded with an English "goodbye," probably one of the few words he knew, waved his hand, and scampered back to his parents.

I was so fascinated by him, even with his teeth missing, that I just stared after him. Suddenly, I wanted to give him something. Remembering that I had a piece or two of gum, I searched my pockets frantically, but when I did find some, my little tow-head with the gorgeous smile had gone. It was as if a spark had died, so much sunshine had he given.

My second trip to the continent was a long taxi ride in an Anson to Brussels, where we stayed overnight. Next morning we continued to a field in Holland, where we collected aircraft to take back to Yorkshire. The weather was lovely going over until we hit Dover, and from there we scooted at 300 feet to Griz-Nez, and then managed to squeeze over the first five miles of French hills until the weather lifted. It was grand then, and Brussels was clear. I had thought for some reason that the city was small and was a bit surprised to find it spreading all over the countryside. The airfield startled me. I expected to see one of those huge, three-runway affairs, and this rather dilapidated, mainly grass field seemed out of place.

There were oodles of planes on the field, ranging from C-47s to Piper Cubs. In fact there was a two-seat P-51 Mustang with a sort of double bubble hood. In the administration building I met a US Navy Commander whom I had known in London. A week later I again saw him in London. Yes, it's a small world! The administration building was large but not particularly well decked out. It had been a pre-war airfield, supposedly one of the best, but even the pre-war "good" airfields of Britain were very poor compared to the war-time super-dupers.

Americans Abroad

People have asked me about my impressions while in Europe and about the boys who are occupying the freed countries. Some of them seemed to be quite happy, if they were located in nice sections, while others were pretty far down in the dumps. Most of them, of course, wanted to go home. There are many areas where the Allies were not welcome, contrary to all Allied propaganda. Some people were well treated by the Germans and prospered. Many people didn't mind the Germans and were annoyed by the Allies, who failed to do as well in business, government, or food distribution. There always seem to be two sides to all questions, and there's always more to a story than you hear about in propaganda.

There were about eight of us, along with our commander, A.D. Pickup. We were always rather amused at his name, especially when he was a taxi pilot "picking up" people. Ann and I sauntered off by ourselves. We first rode into Brussels proper and saw the town mayor. He, or at least his office, gave us permission to stay at the Palace Hotel, a huge building taken over for British officers. This overlooked the big square and even had an open area, with orchestra, as a sort of sidewalk café. These open cafés did get me. Chairs outside, practically forcing pedestrians into the gutter, with customers sipping beer or other drinks and watching the world go by. Definitely continental.

First we signed in at the reception desk and were given room numbers. Then we went to the other side and paid ten francs (20 cents) for our meal tickets. That is, we paid ten francs or twenty cents for a room, dinner that night, breakfast, lunch, and tea the next day! I didn't believe it at first either.

Ann and I went up to a nice double bedroom that had quite decent beds with soft but firm mattresses (we were more unfortunate the next visit we made in getting small cots with unstuffed mattresses). Ann insisted that I taste champagne. So I did, but sad to say, I didn't like it any better than hard drinks. It was sad because the water is not very good, nor is it readily available. The next visit I brought my Boy Scout canteen filled with cold British water, and it quenched my thirst more than once!

We had dinner, not at the hotel but at a NAAFI-run (Navy, Army, and Air Force Institute) hotel across the square. The little French boy, attired in his tuxedo-like waiter's suit, refused at first to let us in, but as usual, if you gesture and push enough, you can enter. We did and found the others waiting for us. Dinner was good, but it stretched out over more than two hours. Ann and I made our escape and walked around to see what we could.

Curfew was at 11:00 PM, so we strode down several streets to find some stores from which we might purchase goods early the next morning. Many were boarded up and there were no shops with particularly fancy displays, because they just didn't have the materials. We felt quite tired, however, when hitting the hay at 10:50. It had been a most enjoyable day.

Ann and I rose early, ate an awful breakfast on our ten-franc bill, and wandered down the shopping center from 9:00 to 10:15. It didn't give us much time, but we procured some down powder puffs, perfume, strawberries, and cherries. The latter two commodities lasted only a short time and my, were they good! A Canadian paratroop captain took us out to the airfield in his big truck, where we all piled into the Anson and settled down to business. That is, we ate nearly all the strawberries and cherries, so that when we arrived to collect the Mosquitoes, we felt quite slap happy.

One after the other, we shot off to the skies and winged our way back to the channel and across to the UK. I wanted to detour over Rotterdam, but I got side-tracked by a Lancaster, with which I flew in loose formation until we had passed by Rotterdam. Lucy Faulkiner had to force land near London when an engine overheated. My plane behaved though, and it was a most enjoyable flight.

Using the radio, I heard lots of jabber, including an inter-plane conversation just as I was heading toward Calais.

"Hello Bubble Two. Hello Bubble Two. Do you hear me? Over."

"Hello Bubble One. Yes, I hear you. Go ahead."

"Hello Bubble Two. Look at that field down there. Sure shot up."

"Yeah, sure is. Must have had a tough time."

"Right. I believe I'm right on course. Now for jolly old England."

"Yippee."

I believe they must have been just behind me but headed directly for London, whereas I was heading to the southwest to Calais and then branching to the northwest to come to the same spot. After about ten minutes I heard them again.

"Hello Bubble Two. Do you hear me? Over."

"Hello Bubble One. Go ahead."

"Hello Bubble Two. There she is, dead ahead." (Probably referring to his landmark in England). "Come to line astern."

"Hello Bubble One. Roger. Over." (Sometimes they used the full correct radio patter, sometimes they didn't.)

A couple of minutes later: "Hello Bubble Two. Let down to 500 feet, but watch that plane coming out of the sun."

"Roger." I strained my eyes looking for them – by the volume through the earphones, I knew they were near and thought perhaps I might be the plane to which they were referring. I didn't spy any other machines. About five minutes later.

"Hello Bubble Two. Park over on the far side. Follow me."

"Roger." And that was the end of one of the millions of trips in this world. Nothing spectacular, just routine.

The third and last trip to the continent was more informal, with no commander around. Ann and I were let out at a small Belgium field west of Brussels at about noon. Since we had tiny, slow Taylorcraft Austers to take and two others had fast Spitfires, they went on with the Anson to Brussels for lunch and a bit of shopping before coming back to start their trips. Ann and I decided we must have some lunch, so we hopped onto a tram (streetcar), and swayed back and forth into the small town. It had been quite badly blitzed, and men and women were still clearing much of the rubble. We went to the main hotel, where Ann had had a very nice lunch before. I was not prepared for what came. First we had our choice of a tomato or mushroom real-egg omelet. I had tomato and Ann had mushroom. The fact that it contained real eggs instead of those never-properly-disguised powered eggs was in itself a treat.

Secondly, I chose beefsteak over veal, thinking of a big hunk of tough and tasteless horsemeat. Instead, out came the most marvelous thick juicy piece of real honest-to-goodness steak! I nearly fainted, for I'd never had one in Britain at any ordinary hotel. The French fries ("chips" in Britain) were crisp, as was the fresh lettuce with real French dressing. I just kept eating long after Ann gave up. When Ann said they had ice cream for dessert, I wondered just what kind of stuff it was. Worth a try anyhow, especially if it were as good as the rest of the meal. So in came my ice cream. Ann just couldn't eat any more. I took one bite and made her order hers – for me. It was the best ice cream I'd had in five years, in the USA or Britain. It had real eggs, real milk, and real vanilla, with the vanilla specks visible. It was rich, creamy, but solid- not icy, not slushy, not over-stocked with fake substances. It was like the old French vanilla of years ago.

Dinner was 200 francs, about a pound ($4.00). It wasn't too expensive, but I'm sure it must have been black market food. Anytime you get an especially good meal, you figure it must be black market. You just don't find that sort of food ordinarily. It didn't bother my conscience, for I couldn't prove whether it was black market or not, the price being quite reasonable. I ate and was satisfied.

After lunch we roamed the streets shopping but didn't buy much. About 4:00 PM we boarded the tram back to the field. Just as we entered the office, we saw the Anson coming in from Brussels. We inquired about the weather and found to our surprise that it had closed in badly over the channel. One RAF lad just came back a few minutes earlier and said it "stank." So we all got back into the Anson and headed for Brussels again to spend the night, as there were no decent sleeping accommodations at this small field.

Back once more to the ten francs (twenty cents) hotel and the square full of strawberries and cherries. We just loafed around, did a tour of the streets, and went to bed. The next morning we did the 9:00-10:15 whirlwind shopping tour and caught a tram back to the field. From Brussels to airfield X to collect our putt-putts. We were a bit worried, as the wind was getting up its dander and the 100-mph Austers would be slowed down to about 70 at 2,000 feet. It was about 75 miles to the coast, so we figured if we reached there in an hour we could get across the straits to Hawkings safely, but if it took longer, we would have to return to a small grass field near our takeoff point. I, being ever cautious, had the RAF boys fill a five-gallon can and prop it beside me, in case I needed to force land and refuel. I don't believe I would have had nerve enough to have done it, but at least I had the gas.

Because of the 35- to 40-mph wind at 2,000 feet, I kept very low and used a lower rpm than recommended to conserve as much gas as

I could. I had no parachute (impossible to wear one in the Auster), so the 100-300 foot altitude level didn't worry me a bit. My map reading was a bit ropey, but I got myself straightened out okay. I hit Calais in exactly an hour and circled for the look-out man to see me. There was no airfield, only a hut on top of a small hill where a man telephoned each Auster going across. If the Auster didn't arrive at Hawkings within a certain safety limit, the Air-Sea Rescue squad was called to search over the particular magnetic course. This hut was hard to find- in fact, I missed it completely- but rather than waste time, I just circled a couple of times, hoping he would see me, and then set out across the 28 miles of water from Calais to Hawkings, south of Dover.

I was still flying low, but the water looked much more uninviting than the rolling hills of France. I gulped a couple of times, felt my Mae West tied securely around me, waved at the men on a freight boat over which I passed by no more than 25 feet, and hoped that the stratus clouds I saw in the distance weren't solid. There was just nothing ahead but water and low clouds. I kept glancing at my watch, and the minutes ticked off slowly, 10, 11, 12. Oh, how slowly time passes over water! Ah, land ahead! I could see the cliffs of Dover on my left, which meant that I had drifted too far north, and I also saw some low cloud covering the tops of the cliffs. Fortunately they were broken, and I managed to get on top to the north and then turn south inland. Hawkings was a welcome relief. Just as I circled, an Auster took off, and I guessed correctly that it was Ann.

However, the trip was only partly over. Refueling, checking in at the Customs, starting up, and another forty minutes of flying. There we waited for a taxi plane, and just as we were to take off, a Spitfire made a tight circuit and landed. We figured it was Big Bill. It seemed that he had gone south of Cherbourg, picked up a Spitfire, flown over 300 miles to where we had taken off, collected another Spit, and just made it back – all in one day, whereas we took all day from Brussels to airfield X to airfield Z in Britain. One certainly gets around these days!

At Aston Down I had my last new type, my 50th – the Hawker Tempest, a very fast single-engine fighter similar to the Typhoon. Inside and outside it looked like the Typhoon, except for the petrol cocks, thinner wings, and tapered rudder. The flying characteristics were quite similar too, except for the landing, where the stick had to be handled just like a Cub. (I dislike the wording "like a Cub." Nothing handles quite like a Cub.)

However, the actual touchdown in a Tempest differed from the usual not-quite-back stick technique in most military aircraft. The Tempest definitely had to have a hard jerk right back in one's tummy before the tail would go down. A real jerk too. You could feel it when you almost had it back, and the elevator became sluggish. If you left the last tug until too late, the tail would stay put, and away you would bounce. Once you get the hang of it though, it was a pleasant feeling. In the air, it felt smoother and nicer than a Typhoon. With the 2,400-horsepower Napier Sabre engine, the pull of the engine was terrific, and you really felt the acceleration.

We flew on a lovely day right over the heart of London (no balloons now), following the great Thames River east to its entry into the channel. The river made a shining spectacle; it's no wonder that German bombers were able to bomb London so well in 1939-1940. The aircraft was cruising at over 300 mph, but I managed to get a glimpse of Hyde Park, Berkeley Square, the Houses of Parliament, and St. Paul's – then I was far beyond it all. I overshot my destination and had to backtrack. At 300 mph or so, it doesn't take long to get from A to B!

Back in April, quite a number of the American ATA pilots returned home. Their American contracts had expired, and they decided not to sign the British contract, which provided a bit less money. Opal Anderson and Grace Stevenson called it quits, as well as ol' "Alabama" Dunleavy, husky and strong, who crushed every gal's ribs; Steffie; Harry Smith, my check-out instructor; Don Richardson; Bill Somogy, the 5'5" kidding champion who wore a tight black beret while flying; and some others whom I had not known.

That left only about half a dozen men and about 10 gals from America. By July 31ˢᵗ, there were only about a dozen altogether. The men expected to be released in September, and several of the American gals' contracts were expiring. Even the British contingent dwindled quickly after May, for the RAF began to do more ferrying. In July, they took over most maintenance units and factories, and by November 30, 1945, the ATA was expected to cease as an organization. Many resigned in order to have a bit of a holiday before going back to their old work or finding a new job.

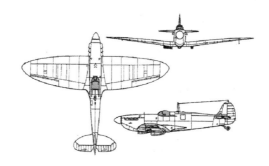

Nancy Miller
Air Transport Auxiliary
Britain, 1942-45

50 types of aircraft flown as pilot in command (single-engines: 35; twin-engines: 15)

Trainers: 7	
Magister	Martinet
Master	Hawker Hart
AT-6 Harvard	Hawker Hind
Tiger Moth	
Fighters (RAF): 6	
Hurricane	Tempest
Spitfire	Gauntlet (1930's fighter)
Typhoon	P-51 Mustang (US)
"Taxi" (transport to and from flights): 1	
Fairchild 24	

Fighters, Fleet Air Arm (Navy), dive bombers, etc.: 12	
Seafire (Navy model Spitfire)	Fulmar
Swordfish	Seamew (US)
Firefly	Wildcat (F4F – US)
Barracuda	Hellcat (F6F – US)
Battle	Corsair (F4U – US)
Albacore	Avenger (TBM – US)

Observation and other types: 9	
Lysander	Puss Moth
Auster (Taylorcraft in US)	Stinson Reliant (US)
Courier	Walrus (amphibious)
Defiant	Sea Otter (amphibious)
Proctor	

"Light" twin-engine: 3	
Oxford	
Anson	
Dominie	

"Heavy" twin-engine: 12	
Wellington	Beaufighter
Lockheed Hudson A-29 (US)	Blenheim
Albemarle	Warwick
Mitchell B-25 (US)	Boston A-20 (US)
Lockheed Ventura B-34 (US)	DeHavilland Mosquito
Hampden	Douglas C-47/DC-3 (US)

(Notes:

"US" designates the American variant of the aircraft. In some cases the RAF flew American-made aircraft, and we ferried them just as we did the British-built aircraft.

Regarding amphibious aircraft, I did not perform water landings during ferry flights.

This list does not include many models and variants of these main types. Special booklets and handling notes gave the necessary information to fly whatever aircraft were assigned. There were no co-pilots, except non-pilot flight engineers in the Mitchell and Dakota.)

Anson C19

Another look at the Beaufighter

Blenheim Bomber

C-47 Dakota (military version of the Douglas DC-3)

Fairey Firefly

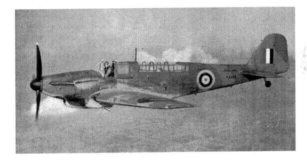

Fairey Fulmar

Seamew AS1

MK1 Defiant

RAF Percival Proctor III

Fairey Swordfish

Supermarine Walrus

De Havilland Puss Moth

Harvard AT-6

XVI.

CONTRACT TERMINATED

Aston Down closed down June 30, 1945, and that meant we all had to be shifted to other pools. Since my contract only ran until July 9th, they shot me to headquarters at White Waltham, where I did two taxi trips and my last delivery in ATA before starting a very boring wait for a boat back home. I had made a round of the country during my three years. First, Luton (north of London), then White Waltham (west of London), then Southampton, Scotland, Aston Down near Bristol, then back to White Waltham.

Because of a rumor that there might be a boat sailing on the 9th or 11th of July, I was given a day off to get my passport and exit permit in order. An army could be mobilized to take care of the queues in the exit permit office! Such disorder and waiting. Not enough staff; certainly not enough patience by either employers or applicants even after I waited hours for nothing. I was lucky though – I had my passport fixed in an hour and got my permit by 5:00 PM, even though it usually takes two to three weeks.

On July 7th I had a Mosquito 35 delivery, my last one. The plane itself wasn't very pleasant, but nothing went wrong. Just before my takeoff, as I was doing my check, a test pilot in a new Hornet, just off the secret list, did some aerobatics for some cameramen. I nearly cricked my neck watching him going straight up – my neck gave way before he rolled out level! It was certainly a marvelous, fast plane and, like all ferry pilots, I wished I could fly one.

However, it was just one more aircraft. I lined up, put Hornet thoughts out of my mind, and roared off. That is, I staggered off, because the throttles wouldn't go fully open, and I had just enough power to pull off. It was no fun! Forty minutes later, I landed nicely and safely, and put it to bed. The good 'ol Mossie – I'll miss her, regardless of that less-than-comfortable last ferry flight.

On July 8th, operations gave me a taxi job in the Fairchild 24. I utilized this last flight to my best advantage. When I arrived to pick up two people and they had not appeared, I promptly went up and practiced 180-degree spot landings and a 360 as the finale. To hell with the gas! It was rough that day, and the woods upset all my calculations. Just when I thought I was right, a downdraft would suck me lower until I had to give power. Or there wasn't the right downdraft, and I'd overshoot. But considering I hadn't practiced very much landing within a 200-foot spot, I thought I did fairly well.

The runway was about 1,800 yards long, and the 200-foot spot looked very small. Hitting that spot three times in a row was the criterion for passing a flight test in the USA. Despite the fact that I supposedly was able to fly any single or twin-engine plane any time solo and deliver it safely, I can't say that I or most of the American pilots who have been away from precision flying for long can take up a light plane and pass a commercial test according to the standard we met four or five years ago.

XVII.

WAITING

Then to London to wait, wait, wait, which is expensive. Living at the Red Cross isn't too bad, but window shopping is dangerous. Edith and I often went out, and we tried so hard to avoid buying anything because of the high prices. One day we walked into Goldsmith's and Silversmith's in Regent Street. We both were looking around for small aircraft models, perched on onyx ashtrays. We found some, but they just weren't finished perfectly. Suddenly, I spied a beautiful Mosquito on the top shelf of the glass showcase.

"Edith," I said slowly, because I knew it would be a terrific price. "Edith, look at THIS!"

Edith did look and then we looked at each other.

"Oh, that's lovely," Edie exclaimed. "I wonder how much it is. Oh, we must look at it." So we had the boy lower it to the counter, where we stared at its beauty with wide-open eyes. It was a magnificent all-silver Mosquito on a rather unusual stand and ebonite box. We both fell in love with it.

"How much is it?" asked Edie, after we had ohhed and ahhed for a while. The man picked up the tag and said "£60." I started sinking through the floor. Edie, in all innocence, remarked brightly, "Oh, £60, why I'd love to have it ….."

"Edie," I interrupted sadly, "£60 is not $60; it's $245." That stopped her. The glow vanished from her eyes, and I knew that we were both looking upon an object far beyond our means. I knew Edie wanted it very much, even more than I did. She had flown many Mosquitoes and liked them so well. It would have been a glorious reminder of the ATA "daze." We sort of stroked the Mossie gently, shook our heads, and sadly walked out.

Edie went to a friend's flat that night and thought about the Mossie. I went back to the Red Cross and thought about it. Finally, sleep put it out of my mind, but the next morning I had a wonderful, brilliant, sudden brainstorm. I dashed down to the shop and put a £5 deposit on it. Being in a spending frenzy, I stopped at another shop and put deposits on three beautiful heavy silver ash trays with etched pictures of London in the middle. In one hour, I had purchased about $300 worth of goods. No wonder I wanted that ship to come in quickly and get us out!

The next day Edith and I had lunch. With her usual curiosity, she wanted to know what I had done in the morning. I managed to stall her, but she suspected something and finally I had to tell her. Poor Edie, who wanted it so much – I felt she'd really get after me! But she just laughed.

"My goodness!" she exclaimed, "I couldn't afford it and am glad you bought it. Now I can visit you and see it. But what in the world suddenly made you decide to buy it? Yesterday, you **kept me** from buying it. I don't know …"

"Well," I sighed, thinking of my very expensive brainstorm, "I just woke up remembering that Dad hadn't sent me anything special for Christmas or my birthday, because he couldn't send much in a five-pound shoe box. He always wants me to have something that I should like. Last summer, when I was home on leave, he let me buy an outfit of clothes on his account for my birthday. So I decided that maybe, since I wanted this Mossie so much, he wouldn't mind giving it to me as a Christmas-birthday gift. It was just a brainstorm, a lovely one. I do hope he doesn't mind too much." Edie shook her head in an "I-don't-know" attitude.

Poor Dad, he just doesn't know what's in store, although I did give him one hint. I sent a cable, understandable taken in its separate sentences but most amusing and disastrous in its whole. Quote: "Still waiting boat. Having good time. Bought myself gift from you. Trust all well." I certainly hope he's well and able to bear the glad news- which I won't tell him until I get up enough nerve. Beautiful Mossie. Poor Dad!!

Edith and I, on our last splurge, delved into the amber shop on Old Bond Street. We looked first, then walked into the shop to inquire about prices – and we were hooked. Edie bought two lovely bracelets, a ring, and earrings, while I bought a pin and a small, gorgeous, three-dimensional Chinese carving of a child's head. My money ran out, so I had to borrow. Owing her a bit over $100, it's no wonder Edie's so anxious that we travel back on the same ship! She has her interest to safeguard!

It didn't take long in London to meet people from the old home state. In fact, for three consecutive nights I met boys who lived very near me, attended Los Angeles High and knew my father. Really too much! Tom Allman and I discussed the idea of being distant cousins, for his aunt was a distant relation of one of my father's cousins or something. The next night, Jerry Doff and I started talking. He went to Los Angeles High and had a scholarship to Occidental College, which I attended for two years. He used to go to a club that met in Dad's church (Dad is the Episcopal minister of St. James Church on Wilshire Blvd.) The next day Edie and Harry were taking in the Tower of London and said they had an ensign also wanting to go, so why not come along? I did. The ensign, it turned out, had been at Los Angeles High two years with me, although we had never met. He often went to hear Dad. I didn't meet anyone from California for a whole week afterwards!

Contact! Britain!

XVIII.

IT'S ALL WORTHWHILE

I am not quite sure how long I will be in England. I can't move because MAP (Ministry of Aircraft Production) might call any time. Therefore I have time to finish this journal. It gives me time to think back over the last three years too. A trip to England, a new country, an education, flying experience never hoped for during peace time, meeting people, a taste of war, confused thoughts, learning patience, rationing, different customs, and ideas- yes, it does give food for thought. It's a shame that a war had to open up such traveling and the resultant learning. But since it did, I am thankful I had the chance to come to Britain.

It might have started out as a lark for many, but the work soon told. If you liked to fly, the job was a very good one but not the safest. The ATA, as a whole, was a better organization to work for than many others. The ATA did give us a chance to help with the war effort, and it also gave us tremendous flight experience.

It was important work, and you could see the results. I recall two Mosquito deliveries a couple of us made to a squadron in northern

Scotland. It was lunch time, so we stopped for a bite to eat before calling for the taxi plane. As we came out and walked back toward the flying control, I heard a fellow behind me mention "828," which was the number of the Mossie I had delivered. I turned around.

"828? You mean the Mosquito that's just been delivered?"

"Yes. Was it yours?" the RAF flight lieutenant asked.

"Sure was. Are you going out to it now?"

"Yeah. Have to make a flight test in it. My ship now."

"Well, it seemed pretty nice to me. Hope you'll like it. Say, by the way," I continued, "how do you like these planes for your work?" He then had his say on the relative merits of the Beaufighter and Mossie for Coastal Command jobs.

"Will you keep this plane now?" I asked.

"Probably. When new ones come in, we have the order in which they are to be distributed. When our turn comes, we usually hold onto it until our next turn."

"It's been nice speaking to you – to deliver a plane to a pilot instead of just to an airfield. It seems more personal and satisfying. And we're glad you want the planes. So many places don't – like MUs and so forth."

"We're certainly glad to see you come in too. That means a new ship for someone and it means a lot to us, you can bet."

The Canadian boy went off to test his new plane. He had served one tour in Coastal Command, instructed in Canada, and then returned as one of the more experienced pilots in the squadron. Because he, as an operational pilot to whom I had delivered my plane, was personally was glad to have it, I was happy. It made up for so many of those dismal flights to the graveyards, dispersal fields, MUs, etc.

Of course, some of the most satisfying flights were into squadron bases where you knew the ships would be used almost immediately. One time I took a Spitfire into a base that had a Polish squadron. While waiting for our taxi aircraft, a Polish pilot came up to me.

"Did you bring in that Spitfire," he asked. "Yes," I replied. "Ah," he said. "Yesterday I was shot down, bailed out over the Channel, and was picked up. Today you have brought me a new Spitfire to fight with. I thank you." Here he was thanking **me**, when **he** was doing the fighting! It was times like these that made our contributions to the war effort seem worthwhile.

There was another time when a whole group of us took Spitfires to a Polish squadron during the busy time just before D-Day. The field had been hastily constructed, and the runways were dirt, covered with wire mesh. The boys lived in tents and ate in tents, and when it rained, everything was all mud. We had lunch with the C.O. and some of the others, and in the afternoon we saw them take off to bomb some railway installations with 500-pound bombs hanging from the fuselages. It was nerve-wracking to watch each Spit as it took off the rough Sommerfield runway, the bombs so close to the ground.

Almost a year later when I attended a Hamble ferry-pool party, the C.O. of that Polish squadron came up to me. He was a quiet, smooth-shaven, nice-looking chap. He remarked:

"Remember that Spitfire you brought in?" I couldn't remember exactly which number it was, naturally, but it had been the only one I had delivered to that squadron.

"I took the Spit you brought in," he continued in his jerky Polish accent. "It was a nice ship. I had good success with it, shot up many railway cars, bombed them, bombed stations and other things. One day the ack-ack got me. The engine quit. Holes were everywhere, although I was still all right. But I was over Germany. I must make France. I crashed but wasn't badly hurt. The Spitfire had brought me home – and, it was your Spitfire," he smiled.

His eyes were friendly. I was so very glad that he and the Spit had made it. All those trains and installations he blew up were a sort of personal contribution from me through him. Those three years meant something then. I wonder what happened to the other planes I delivered—and their wonderfully courageous pilots.

Jackie Cochran (standing) and Helen Richey in the Hurricane fighter

Sue Ford ready to ferry Mosquito bomber

Commander Margot Gore (right) and Flight Captain
Rosemary Rees (2nd in command) of Hamble, Ferry Pool #15

L-R: Helen Harrison, Ann Wood, Sue Ford, Peggy Lennox,
Una Goodwin, 1942 (RAF officer unknown)

Diana Barnato Walker, Faith Bennett with ATA Memorial
plaque, St. Paul's Cathedral, London

Top to bottom: Ann Wood, Sue Ford, Helen Harrison,
Virginia Garst, Grace Stevenson, and Hazel Raines, 1942

L-R: Nancy, Jackie Sorour (So. Africa), Vera Strodl
(Denmark), 1943

Sr. Commander Pauline Gower, commandant of all the
women pilots

Opal Anderson, circa 1943

L-R: Pat Beverley, Barbara McMurray (a flight engineer), Ann Blackwell, Mary Wilkins, and Ann Wood atop a Spitfire.

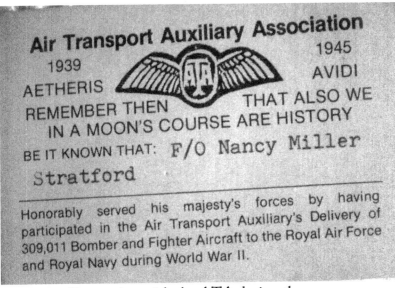

Air Transport Auxiliary Association

1939
1945
AETHERIS
AVIDI
REMEMBER THEN
THAT ALSO WE
IN A MOON'S COURSE ARE HISTORY
BE IT KNOWN THAT: F/O Nancy Miller Stratford

Honorably served his majesty's forces by having participated in the Air Transport Auxiliary's Delivery of 309,011 Bomber and Fighter Aircraft to the Royal Air Force and Royal Navy during World War II.

For serving with the ATA during the war

Helen Harrison (Canadian), 1942

Grace Stevenson (American), 1942

Louise Schuurman (Dutch)

International group relaxing on a "rain-delay" day at Hamble: L-R: Americans Bobbie Leveaux and Emily Chapin on couch at left. Bridge table: Grace Stevenson (at left), Kay Van Doozer (back to camera), Brits Veronica Volkersz (facing), Dora Lang (at right), Ethel Harper (standing, operations), and Doreen Williams center table (facing), with Polish Anna Leska (back to camera). Maureen Dunlop (British, from Argentina), and Margot Duhalde (Chili) are on couch at right. 1943.

Roberta (Bobbie) Sandoz Leveaux and Emily Chapin in "sitcots," the cold-weather attire for open cockpits (e.g., the Tiger Moth).

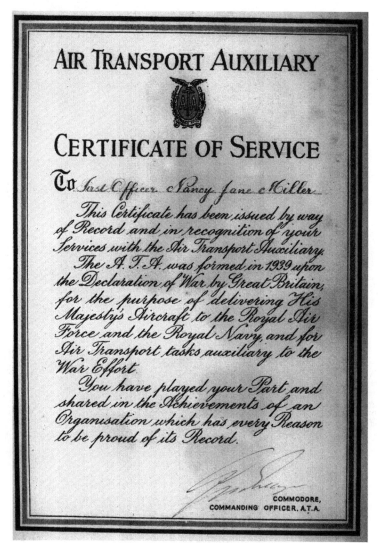

Certificate of Service from the ATA

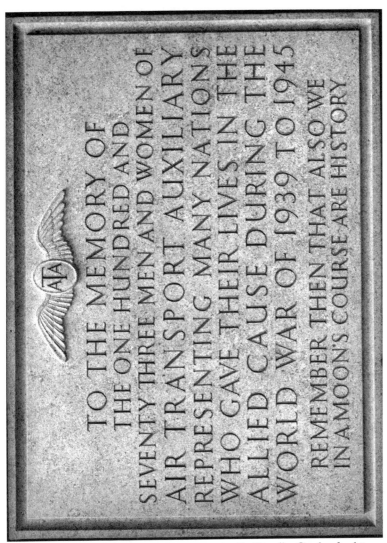

ATA Memorial plaque hanging in St Paul's Cathedral in London, England

Nancy with Sir Edmund Hillary on Mendenhall Glacier,
Juneau, AK, 1963, many years after the "ATA days."

Leather flight helmet, with names of aircraft ferried. I call it
my "BS hat"!

Contact! Britain!

Epilogue

When I've talked with people about flying with the ATA in Great Britain during World War II, I've often been asked, "Why don't you write a book?" or "Have you written a book?" I never thought much about it until 2009, when my friend Ann Wilde said, forcefully, "This is a story that must be told." I didn't think so; my life was nothing spectacular. However Ann kept urging me to write up something, because there were few women pilots at that time. Some people were aware that the Women's Airforce Service Pilots (WASP) had done a fine job in the USA, but many did not know American women were ferrying airplanes in England during the war, working with the British Royal Air Force and Navy.

Ann kept prodding me until I remembered that I had a "book" that I had written in 1945. "Hold on," I said to her one day, "Let me look for this book—not a book, really, but a memoir I wrote about my experience of the war years just after we were demobilized." I found it amongst my other library books, handed it to her, and she read it. I had not looked at it for some 60 years and could not recall what was in it!

The result was that Ann kept insisting I edit and publish this manuscript, in which she had the cooperation and assistance of my niece Peggy. We all poured over it, mainly to correct typos, grammar, and other obvious errors, but the events and terminology are as I remembered them in 1945. This manuscript comprises some of the adventures of just one person; all the American women pilots had different experiences, flew different aircraft, and were based at different pools. So some of the "facts" as I knew them at that time may not be correct—since then I have learned more about that era and about some of the women. But I have left the contents pretty much as I wrote them in 1945.

I thought my adventures might be interesting to my nieces. It would show them what their "crazy ol' Aunt Nan" did during the war. I was fortunate that I was able to do what I loved to do and to feel I had contributed to the war effort.

I continued flying after the war. The end came in 1978, when the engine noises finally affected my hearing to the point that I had to retire. It was a great "run," a wonderful career.

Thanks to Ann, whose insistence kept me going and who helped with the editing, and Peggy, who continued with the transcribing, final editing and a multitude of chores; and Marc, who brought the book to fruition —and my gratitude to all three for their encouragement and support.

I loved all the flying, the freedom, doing what I liked to do. It was "wild and wooly" at times. I was a lucky person in my career. I smile. I have absolutely no regrets

Nancy (Miller) Stratford
Carlsbad, May 2010

Afterword

When Nancy Jane Miller returned to the United States, she had difficulty finding work as a pilot, despite her experience with a remarkable variety of aircraft and her King George VI (1939-45) Service Medal from the British government. At that time, women were being asked, and in many cases required, to cede their jobs to the returning male veterans.

She eventually joined Livingston Air Service and Air Dusting, Inc., in Corvallis, Oregon. Her duties including instructing in ground and flight school, bookkeeping, flying an AT-6 Harvard in air shows, and dusting crops using a Stearman biplane. She also delivered new Piper aircraft from the factory in Pennsylvania to customers in Oregon. Unofficial duties, she tells me, included janitorial services and shoving wood into a big furnace for heating!

In July 1947, Miller earned helicopter and seaplane ratings. She was the first woman on the West Coast to receive a commercial helicopter rating, the second in the US, and the fourth in the world. She flew a Hiller 12B as a flight instructor and was one of the first helicopter crop-duster pilots. She also flew helicopters in air shows, hauled passengers, delivered Santa Claus, flew photo missions and fish counts, and fought wildfires.

Married to Arlo Livingston in 1956, Miller moved with him to Juneau, Alaska, in July 1960; there the couple started a helicopter service, Livingston Copters, Inc. She was the only woman helicopter pilot in the state at the time. She flew Hiller 12Es and Alouette IIs on photo missions, took passengers (including Sir Edmund Hillary) on sightseeing tours over the glaciers, and flew skiers up the mountains. She also served as base radio operator, bookkeeper, administrative assistant, and vice president of Livingston Copters. Since her hearing had been damaged from the roar of airplane engines over the years, she retired in 1978, having flown some 8500 hours in 103 types of aircraft.

Miller has the honor of being Whirly Girl #4. That organization recognizes women pilots across the globe in the order in which they receive their commercial helicopter ratings. She possesses one of the 100 silver medals that Howard Hughes had commissioned on the assumption that there would never be more than 100 female helicopter pilots in the world. There are now over 1400.

Miller is a life member of the 99s, an international woman pilots association named for the 99 women present at the first meeting. She is also a member of the Twirly-Birds and the Silver Wings and served on the first Women's Advisory Committee on Aviation (WACOA) under President Johnson.

Upon her husband's decease, in 1988 Miller requested that the Whirly-Girls establish the Arlo Livingston Award with her sponsorship. Livingston had become a pioneer helicopter pilot during his Alaska years, and he had served as the president of the Helicopter Association International (HAI) and a charter member of the Men's Auxiliary of the Whirly-Girls. The award honors a woman pilot for her contributions on behalf of women in helicopter aviation. The women who have received the award over the years have been some of the most distinguished women pilots in the world. In 2002, the Whirly-Girls presented Miller with a Lifetime Achievement Award for her "contributions over the past 60 years."

In 1991, Miller married Milton Stratford, since deceased, and moved to San Diego, where she now resides. In 2008, Prime Minister Brown and the British Parliamentary Under Secretary of State for Transport invited her and the other 162 remaining ATA personnel (of whom 52 were able to attend) to 10 Downing Street in order to present a long-overdue award for their wartime service, the Air Transport Auxiliary Veterans Badge.

Peg Miller
Carlsbad, May 2010

PHOTOGRAPHY

All photos not belonging to the author were used by permission. In each case, the owner or source of the photo is listed.

P. 30	Map	Author's personal collection
P. 45	Spitfire	Author's personal collection
P. 46-47	Logbook	Author's personal collection
P. 80	Cockpit Illustration	Author's personal collection (origin unknown)
P. 81, 85, 94-95, 99	Various	Author's personal collection
P. 119	Spitfire	Wiki GNU Free Documentation License
	DeHavilland Mosquito	RAF archives- public domain
P. 120	Albacore Fairey	Wiki GNU Free Documentation License
	Hawker Tempest	RAF archives- public domain
P. 121	Bristol Beaufighter	RAF archives- public domain
	Fairey Battle	RAF archives- public domain
P. 122	Hawker Hurricane	RAF archives- public domain
	Hawker Typhoon	RAF archives- public domain
P. 123	Fairchild 24	Wiki GNU Free Documentation License
	Auster	RAF archives- public domain
P. 124	Westland Lysander	RAF archives- public domain
	DeHavilland Dominie	RAF archives- public domain
P. 125	P-51 Mustang	Copyright by Marc C. Lee
	F4U Corsair	Wiki GNU Free Documentation License
P. 126	TBM Avenger	Wiki GNU Free Documentation License
	Grumman Hellcat	USAF historical photo archives

Nancy Miller, first flying lesson. Oakland, CA, 1939

Nancy Miller in 2009

Made in the USA
Lexington, KY
26 February 2011